Bible Studies
for a
Firm Foundation

by Bob and Rose Weiner

"If the foundations are destroyed, what can the righteous do?"
Psalm 11:3

Cover Photograph
by Jerry Sieve

BIBLE STUDIES FOR A FIRM FOUNDATION
TABLE OF CONTENTS

Scripture references in *Bible Studies for a Firm Foundation* are designed for use with the *New American Standard Version*.

THE ATONEMENT
GOD'S PROVISION FOR MAN'S SIN

When God created man, it was His desire to have a family of men and women in His likeness and in His image with whom He could fellowship, share His life, and love. God spent the first five days of creation preparing a home for the sons of His love. The Lord God created all the stars of heaven, the sun and the moon to give light upon the earth for His sons. All the beautiful flowers, trees, mountains, rivers and all the brilliant colors of the world were given and prepared for the enjoyment and pleasure of the men and women whom He would create to be His own. On the sixth day of creation, God made man and woman in His image and gave them the breath of life. And God saw all His creation and acknowledged that it was good. God placed the man and woman He had made in a beautiful garden prepared just for them. Among the trees in the garden were the tree of the knowledge of good and evil and the tree of life. God gave them permission to eat from any tree in the garden, including the tree of life. However, there was one tree from which God commanded them not to eat; for if they ate from it they would die. Notice that God set before His beloved ones a choice of whether to obey God, love Him and live—or to disobey Him, not love Him and die. The God of heaven and earth has never forced man to love Him—or serve Him, but desired that they would love Him and choose Him with their free will and from their heart.

1. What did Adam and Eve choose to do? (Gen. 3:3-6)

_____

We see that Adam and Eve chose not to love God and obey Him, but they chose to rebel against God and disobey Him.

2. What was the secret motive of their heart? (Gen. 3:5; Isa. 14:13-14)

_____

This is the basic sin of all men. Each has tried to be his own god and exalt his will above God's will.

3. On what three things were Adam and Eve's sin based? (Gen. 3:6; I John 2:16)
   a _____
   b _____
   c _____

The lust of the flesh, the lust of the eyes and the boastful pride of life are the root causes to all sin in this world.

4. What do we find God doing in the garden, and what was the desire of His heart? (Gen. 3:8-9)

_____

The God of heaven and earth came to the garden to fellowship with the sons of His love and to share His heart with them, finding only that they had broken His commandment and had gone their own independent way. By turning away from God in disobedience, man lost the blessing and protection of God and came under a curse and the power of the devil. They were cast out of the garden losing their fellowship with the Father. Because of Adam and Eve's transgression, the knowledge of good and evil has come to all men; every unregenerate man has desires bent toward sin.

5. What does the Scripture teach about the spiritual condition of a man who willfully sins against God? (Rom. 3:10-19, 23)

a (v. 10) _____

b (v. 11) _____

c (v. 11) _____

d (v. 12) _____

e (v. 12) _____

f (v. 13-14) _____

g (v. 15) _____

h (v. 16) _____

i (v. 17) _____

j (v. 18) _____

k (v. 23) _____

6. If all have sinned willfully and are *not* seeking God, then how can men come to God? (Isa. 19:20; Luke 19:10; John 6:44)

_____

_____

7. Therefore what is it that brings men to repentance? (Rom. 2:4)

_____

It is the love and kindness of God that goes out and seeks rebellious men. It is the love of God that strives with the heart of men convicting them of sin and drawing them to Himself. It is the love of God that continues to push the stubborn and rebellious man into a corner until he gives up and surrenders his life of sin and death. Yet, God has given every man a free will to choose Him and live or to reject His provision and die.

8. Can we save ourselves by our own good works? (Eph. 2:8-9; Titus 3:5)

_____

9. Can we be saved by keeping the law? (Gal. 3:21; Rom. 3:20)

_____

10. What was Paul's testimony about himself in regard to the law and to sin? (Phil. 3:6; I Tim. 1:15)

_____

11. What was the purpose of the law? (Rom. 3:19-20)

_____

12. Under the Old Covenant, how was a man cleansed from sin and brought into a right relationship with God? (Lev. 17:11)

_____

The blood sacrifice as the atonement and covering for sin was instituted by God from the beginning of time. Adam, Abel, Noah, Abraham, Jacob and finally the nation of Israel all offered blood sacrifices for the atonement of sin. God required animal sacrifices, for their blood is pure, innocent and undefiled; it is free from the nature bent toward sin. Under the Old Covenant, the shedding of this blood brought a covering and atonement for man's sin.

13. What did Jesus come to do? (Matt. 1:20-23; I John 3:5)

_____

14. What was said of Him? (John 1:29)

_____

The blood line comes from the father. The Bible tell us that the life of the flesh is in the blood. In Jesus there was no sin. He was *not* born from Adam. The blood of God ran through Jesus' veins, and it was that blood which was shed for the sins of the world.

15. Is the blood of Jesus a better sacrifice than the blood of animals? (Heb. 9:13-14)

_____

The atonement that Jesus made was greater than the atonement under the Old Covenant. His atonement was more than just an offering for the forgiveness of sins, because the forgiveness of sins was available through the blood of animals under the Old Covenant.

16. What did Jesus actually do for us on the cross? (I Peter 2:24; Gal. 3:13; Rom. 6:6-7)
   a _____
   b _____
   c _____
   d _____

Consequently, we see that the atonement of Jesus not only provided forgiveness but brought complete deliverance from sin, sickness and the curse.

17. What is the "New Covenant" that Jesus established and made available through His blood? (Heb. 8:8-12; Ezk. 36:26-27)
   a (v. 10) _____
   b (v. 10) _____
   c (v. 11) _____
   d (v. 12) _____
   e (v. 26) _____
   f (v. 26) _____

18. How can we become partakers of this New Covenant? (Acts 3:19; Rom. 10:9-10)
   a _____
   b _____

_____

19. Why did Jesus come? (John 3:16-17)

_____

20. Who is under God's judgment? (John 3:18-19)

_____

If men reject God's provision for them under the New Covenant through Jesus the Messiah, there is no way they can be saved; for there is no other atonement apart from the cross of Jesus Christ.

21. What is the final end of all unrepentant sinners? (Matt. 25:41; Rev. 20:12-15)

_____

22. What is God's desire? (II Peter 3:9)

_____

MEMORY VERSES: Rom. 5:9; Gal. 1:4

_____

_____

_____

_____

_____

REPENTANCE
THE LORDSHIP OF JESUS
THE MESSIAH

1. In preaching the gospel to the Jews, what did Peter say about Jesus? (Acts 2:36)

   _____

2. When the Jews heard this preaching, what happened and what was their response? (Acts 2:37)

   _____

3. What did Peter say that they must do? (Acts 2:38)

   a _____

   b _____

   c _____

In this series we will deal separately with each of these three basic truths. The first one we shall consider is repentance.

4. How does the Word of God define repentance? (Ps. 32:3-5; Prov. 28:13; Ezk. 18:21-23, 27-28)

   _____

   _____

5. If we confess our sins, what will God do? (I John 1:9; Isa. 1:18, 20)

   _____

   _____

6. In repentance what else must we be willing to do? (Ezk. 33:15)

   _____

This *restitution* must be made as the Spirit of God instructs and leads. Zaccheus, being a Jew, was familiar with this teaching of repentance and restitution by the prophet Ezekiel. Zaccheus was a very wicked man, a tax collector; and had treated many men unjustly.

7. When Jesus said to Zaccheus that He would come to his house, what was Zaccheus' response that showed his repentant heart? (Luke 19:1-8)

   _____

   _____

8. What did Jesus say to Zaccheus? (Luke 19:9-10)

   a _____

   b _____

9. What conditions does God set for receiving us and being a Father to us? (II Cor. 6:14-18)

   a _____

   b _____

   c _____

This condition for repentance is demonstrated very clearly in a parable of Jesus about a lost son.

10. What had the lost son done? (Luke 15:11-16)

   _____

This is a picture of those who are involved in worldliness and sin.

11. What did the lost son decide to do when he realized his state? (Luke 15:17-19)

_____

Notice that there had to be a decision on his part to come out from the world and be separate and to go to his father's house.

12. As soon as the son had made the decision in his heart to separate himself from the unclean thing and to go to his father to confess his sin, what did the father do? (Luke 15:20)

_____

13. The son was hoping only to be allowed to become a hired servant of the father, yet what did the father make him? (Luke 15:22-24)

_____

So also will the Heavenly Father do for us as it is written:

> _"Come out from their midst and be separate," says the Lord,_
> _"and do not touch what is unclean;_
> _and I will welcome you. And I will be a Father to you,_
> _and you shall be sons and daughters to Me,"_
> _says the Lord Almighty._
> _— II Cor. 6:17-18_

14. We see this same requirement made of the Israelites when they were going in to possess the land that God had given them. What did God require of them in regard to the heathen nations? (Deut. 7:1-3)

    a _____

    b _____

    c _____

15. Why did God require this? (Deut. 7:4,6; Deut. 8:1)

    a _____

    b _____

    c _____

We too have a spiritual land to possess and very real spiritual enemies to overcome.

16. God has always desired a holy people for His own possession. To what does God compare this relationship between the Messiah and His church? (Eph. 5:25-32)

_____

17. Describe God's attitude toward this marriage covenant. (Isa. 62:4-5)

_____

18. When Israel went astray from her covenant with God, what was she called by God? (Hosea 9:1; 4:12)

_____

Any breaking of this covenant and going astray from this commitment is referred to by the Lord as harlotry and adultery.

19. What three things does James say about those who have friendship with the ways of the world? (James 4:4)

    a _____

    b _____

    c _____

20. What is the Lord's attitude toward His bride? (James 4:5)

_____

21. If anyone loves the ways of the world, what does John say about him? (I John 2:15)

_____

22. What is in the world? (I John 2:16)

a _____

b _____

c _____

23. What happens to those who do the will of God? (I John 2:17)

_____

24. What commandment did Jesus give for us to follow, and what did He say for us to seek first? (Mark 12:28-31; Matt. 6:33)

a _____

b _____

25. What must a man do in order to be a disciple of Jesus? (Luke 14:26-33)

_____

Briefly summarized, we can say that unless a man is willing to *forsake* all that he has he cannot be a disciple of Jesus. The first command is this, "Thou shalt have no other gods before me." To hate your parents, friends, relatives and even your own life means that you do not exalt your love for them or their opinions—or even your own opinions—above the will of God.

26. Therefore, before we decide to become a disciple and follower of Jesus, what are we exhorted to do? (Luke 14:28-30)

_____

In the parable of the rich young ruler, we see this truth beautifully demonstrated.

27. What did the rich young ruler want? (Matt. 19:16)

_____

Jesus' response was that he should keep the commandments.

28. What was the young ruler's response? (Matt. 19:20)

_____

Notice that although the rich young ruler had been morally good and obedient he still recognized that his relationship with God was not right and was lacking.

29. What requirement did Jesus make of him? (Matt. 19:21)

_____

Jesus put His finger on this man's idolatry, upon his god—the thing he was truly serving.

30. What action by the rich young ruler proved that he was serving another god? (Matt. 19:22)

_____

Notice that Jesus did not run after this man to make a compromise or to give him another chance. The first and greatest commandment is this, "You shall love the Lord your God and Him *only* shall you serve." Anything less than this is not acceptable and is nothing less than idolatry.

31. What will the Lordship of Jesus bring? (Matt. 10:34)

_____

Jesus came to make peace between a man and his God, yet in a world that is at enmity with Him, conflict will arise.

32. What does Jesus point out as the three main areas of this conflict? (Matt. 10:17-22, 35-36)

a _____

b _____

c _____

33. What did Paul say we must do to be saved? (Rom. 10:9)

a _____

b _____

To confess that someone is your Lord and Master means that you are committing your entire life to that person to be his slave for life; you are committing your own will and desires to him to do his bidding.

34. What shall those who have forsaken all to follow Him receive? (Matt. 19:27-29; Mark 10:29-30)

a _____

b _____

c _____

35. To as many as receive Him what does Jesus give? (John 1:12)

_____

36. If we open our hearts to receive Jesus, what promise has He given us? (Rev. 3:20)

_____

37. What experience do we have as a result? (John 3:3-7)

_____

38. When we receive Jesus, what does God give us through Him? (I John 5:11; Rom. 6:23)

_____

MEMORY VERSE: (II Cor. 6:17-18)

_____

_____

_____

_____

BAPTISM IN WATER

When we come to Jesus and repent of our sins, we enter into what the Bible calls the "born again" experience. We experience a "new birth" and receive a new heart. Jesus comes to dwell in our hearts by faith. We become partakers of eternal life, for eternal life is in the Son. When we depart from this life, we shall go to be with the Lord.

1. What are three vital elements of the Christian life? (Acts 2:38)

   a _____

   b _____

   c _____

In our previous studies we have discussed the atonement of Jesus and God's provision for man's sins. We have discussed what true repentance and submission to the Lordship of Jesus means. We come now to our next truth, water baptism, in which we experience a burial of our old nature and a rising to walk with Christ in newness of life. Water baptism in itself is not effectual for salvation.

2. What did Jesus Himself say? (Matt. 28:19)

   _____

Let us now examine additional Scriptures concerning the significance of water baptism.

3. For what purpose was our old sin-loving nature crucified with Him? (Rom. 6:6)

   a _____

   b _____

> "We know that our old (unrenewed) self was nailed
> to the cross with Him in order that (our) body,
> (which is the instrument) of sin, might be made
> ineffective and inactive for evil, that we might
> no longer be the slaves of sin."
> —Rom. 6:6 Amplified Version

4. What provision did Jesus make for the putting off of the sin-loving nature? (Col. 2:11)

   _____

5. What is the circumcision of Christ? (Col. 2:11-12)

   _____

This circumcision, made without hands, is a supernatural work of God. In a sense, in the waters of baptism, God supernaturally takes His scalpel and cuts away from our life the bondage to sin and buries it. A tremendous deliverance and victory takes place.

6. What was circumcision a sign of under the Old Covenant? (Gen. 17:10-11)

   _____

7. What happened to those who were not circumcised and why? (Gen. 17:13-14)

   a _____

   b _____

8. With whom did God establish this covenant of circumcision? (Gen. 17:19)

   _____

9. From whom are we descended as the children of promise? (Rom. 9:6-8)

   _____

10. Whom did Paul say were the true circumcision? (Phil. 3:3)

_____

11. How did Moses, prophetically speaking of the New Covenant, describe this true circumcision? (Deut. 30:6)

_____

Let us look at another Old Testament example. After forty years of wandering, the generation of disobedient Israelites, whom God had originally brought out of Egypt, died in the wilderness. When the Lord rolled back the waters of the Jordan River just as He had done at the Red Sea, this new generation walked through the Jordan River and into the promised land.

12. What was the first thing that they did? (Josh. 5:2)

_____

13. Why did they do it? (Josh. 6:5-7)

_____

14. What did the Lord say that He did when they were circumcised? (Josh. 5:9)

_____

Before the Israelites could go up and possess the promised land, they had to be circumcised so that the reproach of Egypt might be rolled away from them. That circumcision was a sign in their flesh of their covenant with God. So also, under the New Covenant before we can go up and possess our promised inheritance, we must receive the circumcision of Jesus, made without hands, in putting off the "body of the sins of the flesh". Through this circumcision we are uprooted from the world, of which Egypt is a picture, and the reproach of the world is rolled away from us.

15. What then is circumcision in the New Covenant? (Col. 2:11-13)

_____

Circumcision in the natural sense is the cutting away of the unclean part, the foreskin of the man. In the spiritual sense, circumcision is a cutting away of the whole body of sins, the sin-loving nature. Even more, baptism is a burial and resurrection, a total dying of the old self by union with Christ, a real and present rising again by participation in His risen life.

Another beautiful picture of water baptism is found in the Old Testament. It is a type and shadow of the meaning of baptism under the New Covenant. The Israelites had been held in bondage in Egypt for many years. They had been enslaved to Pharaoh, the cruel king. When the Lord brought them forth from bondage in the Exodus, He parted the Red Sea before them. The water was like a wall on either side of them as the Israelites passed through to the other side. Pharaoh and his armies, who were pursuing Israel, followed them into the water. The Lord, however, caused the water to roll back together cutting the Egyptians off and causing them to drown.

The ones who held Israel in bondage and slavery in Egypt, who were pursuing her in her new relationship with God, were buried in the waters of the Red Sea. Israel was left alone on the other side of the water free from slavery, free to be servants of their God. If the sea had not buried the Egyptians, the threat of slavery would have followed them into the promised land. Not only would Israel have had to fight her enemies in the promised land, but she would have had to fight the one who was trying to bring her back into bondage. Those who have come to faith in Christ and are identified with Him through water baptism have been made free from the power and bondage of sin and have pressed on into the promised land able to meet and conquer their enemies head on.

16. In fact, what does Paul say about Israel's experience at the Red Sea? (I Cor. 10:1-2)

_____

17. When believers are baptized, they are following Jesus in what experience of His? (Rom. 6:4)

a _____

b _____

18. If we have been united with Him in the likeness of His death, what shall we also be? (Rom. 6:5)

_____

19. Jesus partook of our flesh and blood and died. Why did He do this? (Heb. 2:14-15)

   a _____

   b _____

As He hung on the cross, Jesus became sin on our behalf (II Cor. 5:21). The purpose of this was to bring us to God the Father. Jesus died on the cross to make a perfect atonement for man's sinful and lost condition. On the third day He arose from the dead and triumphed over Satan, thereby providing for man's salvation. Because we receive His life when we make Jesus Lord, our relationship to God is made alive and we also live in fellowship with God. Likewise, as we partake in water baptism, we share Jesus' burial and resurrection. Because we now share the resurrection life of Jesus, sin no longer has dominion over us.

Now that we have established the Scriptural meaning of baptism, let us look into the Scriptural application of it.

20. How did the people act who received the Word of God? (Acts 2:41)

_____

21. What did the people of Samaria do after they believed Philip's teaching? (Acts 8:12)

_____

22. What did the Ethiopian eunuch desire after he had heard the message of Philip about the Messiah? (Acts 8:35-36)

_____

23. In what way, or by what method, was the eunuch baptized? (Acts 8:38-39)

_____

The baptisms throughout the New Testament, including the baptisms of John, were all done by immersion— the people all went down into the water and came up again. The water represents the grave where the burial takes place.

24. What did the Philippian jailer do after believing Paul's message? (Acts 16:29-33)

_____

25. When was he baptized? (Acts 16:33)

_____

26. When were those who heard Peter's message baptized? (Acts 2:41)

_____

Notice the immediacy of all the baptisms recorded in the book of Acts. Likewise, there should be no delay in the baptism of believers today.

27. In what name did Jesus tell the disciples to baptize? (Matt. 28:19)

_____

28. In what name did the disciples baptize? (Acts 2:38; Acts 8:14-16; Acts 10:45-48; Acts 19:5)

_____

We read in Colossians 2:9: "For in Him all the fulness of Deity dwells in bodily form." Jesus' disciples understood this; for having His command, they went everywhere baptizing new believers. They were baptizing in the name which is above all names, in the name which all authority of heaven and earth is invested, and that name is Jesus. In the name of Jesus, demons are cast out, the sick are healed, and the lame walk.

29. Into whom are we baptized? (Rom. 6:3)

_____

30. Many believers have gone through the motions of baptism, yet have not experienced a genuine New Testament baptism. What have they experienced? (Acts 19:3-4)

_____

In the Old Testament, an account is given of Naaman, the captain of the army of the King of Syria, who had leprosy. He went to Elisha, the prophet of God, to ask for healing. Leprosy in the Scripture is a type of the "body of sins of the flesh" or of the bondage of the power of sin because there is no cure for this disease apart from the mercy of God. The whole flesh is infected, and the end of it is death.

31. What did Elisha tell him to do? (II Kings 5:9-10)

_____

32. What was his response? (II Kings 5:11-12)

_____

Likewise, many people are insulted by God's command for water baptism, thinking it is silly and ridiculous.

33. What was the servant's advice to him, and what did he do? (II Kings 5:13-14)

_____

_____

_____

Likewise, we must become as little children and obey the simple things that God asks us to do. His ways are far above our ways. We must lean not to our own understanding. We must be careful lest we only desire to do great feats for God yet are not willing to humble ourselves to God's way of doing things.

MEMORY VERSE: Col. 2:11-12

_____

_____

_____

_____

BAPTISM IN THE HOLY SPIRIT

1. What instruction did Peter give to the Jewish people who were under conviction following his sermon at Pentecost? (Acts 2:37-38)

   a _____

   b _____

   c _____

2. What did Jesus tell His disciples to do before they went out into the world to preach repentance? (Luke 24:47-53)

   _____

   _____

3. What was the "promise of the Father" they were to receive? (Acts 1:4-5)

   _____

4. What did Jesus say would happen when the Holy Spirit came upon them? (Acts 1:8)

   _____

Notice that this empowering produces the ability to *be* a witness; that is, it gives the ability to live the Christian life and the power to preach the gospel.

5. How did Jesus fulfill His ministry? (Acts 10:38)

   _____

6. What type of proof had the disciples been given of Jesus' resurrection? (Acts 1:3)

   _____

   _____

It is interesting to notice that although the disciples had been taught by Jesus over a period of three years, had seen the resurrected Messiah in all His glory and power over a period of 40 days, and had fellowshipped intensely with Him, they were not allowed to go and preach the Gospel until *after* they had received the baptism of the Holy Spirit and had been clothed with power from on High. Yet, how many "born again" believers attempt to go and preach the Gospel without it?

7. What did Jesus say about the Holy Spirit that He would send? (John 14:16-17)

   _____

8. What are two other names for the Holy Spirit? (John 14:16-17)

   a _____

   b _____

9. What other things did Jesus tell the disciples that the Holy Spirit would do for them? (John 14:26; John 15:26; John 16:13)

   a _____

   b _____

   c _____

   d _____

   e _____

10. Paul also speaks of this empowering. What did he say about the Gospel which he preached? (I Cor. 2:4)

   _____

11. On what should the faith of men not rest? (I Cor. 2:5)

_____

12. On what should their faith rest? (I Cor. 2:5)

_____

13. How did Paul say that we might know the things that God has given us? (I Cor. 2:9-12)

_____

14. What did Jesus say the Spirit would do for us when we are delivered up before the governors, kings and those in authority? (Matt. 10:18-20)

_____

15. Consequently, what are we exhorted to do when we are delivered up for the defense of the Gospel? (Matt. 10:19)

_____

16. What are two other names for the Holy Spirit? (Matt. 10:20; Gal. 4:6)

a _____

b _____

All these benefits are available to all believers when the Holy Spirit is received.

17. Besides the eleven apostles, who else was waiting to receive the promise of the Holy Spirit? (Acts 1:13-15)

_____

18. What was the total number present? (Acts 1:15)

_____

19. Although these people were staying in the upper room for lodging purposes, where were they continually meeting to praise the Lord? (Luke 24:52-53)

_____

20. During this time, because of the Feast of Pentecost, who was present at Jerusalem and in the temple? (Acts 2:5)

_____

21. What happened when the Holy Spirit was given? (Acts 2:1-4)

a _____

b _____

c _____

22. What happened when this sound occurred? (Acts 2:6)

_____

This out-pouring of the Holy Spirit did not take place in a small room somewhere behind locked doors. This thing was not done in a corner but in the temple before the eyes of all Israel.

23. How did Peter explain what was happening? (Acts 2:14-21)

_____

24. What did the tongues of fire that rested upon the believers represent? (Matt. 3:11-12)

_____

This fire of the Holy Spirit represents the cleansing and purifying work of the Spirit in the lives of believers.

25. How does John describe this cleansing work? (Matt. 3:12)

_____

_____

26. The prophet Malachi speaks of these cleansing fires. Describe this refining and purifying work that is to be done by the Holy Spirit. (Mal. 3:1-3)

_____

_____

This cleansing and purifying work does not take place overnight. It is a process that only begins when we are baptized with the Holy Spirit. A refiner of silver heats the silver over a burning fire. As the silver becomes hot, all the dross and impurities rise to the top. He then skims off the impurities. He continues heating and skimming off the dross again and again until he can see his image reflected clearly in the silver. So also the Holy Spirit through trials and tests skims all the dross and impurities from our lives that the image of Jesus may be seen in us.

27. In fact, what does Paul say the Spirit of the Lord has come to do? (II Cor. 3:18)

_____

28. How did the Gentiles receive the Holy Spirit? (Acts 10:44-45)

_____

29. How did they know the Gentiles had received the Holy Spirit? (Acts 10:45-46)

_____

30. How did the believers at Samaria receive the Holy Spirit? (Acts 8:17)

_____

31. How did the believers at Ephesus receive the Holy Spirit? (Acts 19:6)

_____

32. What happened when they received the Holy Spirit? (Acts 19:6)

_____

33. What does the prophet Ezekiel say about the Holy Spirit when he is prophesying about the New Covenant? (Ezk. 36:26-27)

_____

34. To whom is the promised gift of the Holy Spirit made available? (Acts 2:39)

_____

_____

35. To whom will the Father give the Holy Spirit? (Luke 11:13)

_____

_____

MEMORY VERSE: Acts 2:38-39

_____

_____

_____

_____

—NOTES—

THE HOLY SPIRIT—THE GIFT OF GOD

1. What does Peter say that the Holy Spirit is? (Acts 2:38)

   _____

2. What does Paul say about the significance of the promised Holy Spirit that is given to us as believers? (Eph. 1:13-14)

   _____

   _____

The Holy Spirit is a pledge or an engagement ring of promise. It is given to us as a promise from God that He will redeem us completely—body, soul and spirit. It is a promise of full redemption in order that we might be a holy and perfect dwelling place for God in the Spirit so that we might be transformed into the very image of Jesus. The degree to which we are controlled by the Spirit of God at the beginning of our Christian walk is but a mere seed of what will one day flood our whole being and cause those who go on to know the Lord to be filled with the fulness of "resurrection life."

The Amplified Bible says it this way:

> *"That Spirit is the guarantee of our inheritance—the firstfruit,*
> *the pledge and foretaste, the down payment of our heritage—*
> *in anticipation of its full redemption and our acquiring*
> *complete possession of it."*
> *—Eph. 1:14*

3. What is eternal life? (John 17:3)

   _____

4. What spirit have we received? (Rom. 8:15)

   _____

5. To what does the Spirit within us bear witness? (Rom. 8:16)

   _____

6. Who are the sons of God? (Rom. 8:14)

   _____

The Baptism in the Holy Spirit is the gateway into a life filled with fellowship and communion with the Father. It is the turning point from being enslaved to the spirit in this age and our fleshly desires to being under the power of God's Spirit. Through the Spirit's power, we may press on in God toward the fulness of resurrection life.

In our previous study, we found that besides bringing a revelation of Jesus, the Holy Spirit was given to empower us for effective witness and service. We shall now turn our thoughts toward the different gifts and graces that are resident in the gift of the Holy Spirit, and that are available to us as believers.

7. What are a few of the glorious things that happened through the early church under the anointing of the Holy Spirit? (Acts 3:1-10; Acts 8:5-7; Acts 9:36-42)

   a _____

   b _____

   c _____

   d _____

8. How did Jesus Himself minister and preach to those in need? (Luke 4:18)

   _____

9. How did Jesus cast out demons? (Matt. 12:28)

   _____

10. What signs did Jesus say would follow all those who believe? (Mark 16:17)

    a _____

    b _____

    c _____

    d _____

    e _____

11. What did the Lord confirm with these signs? (Mark 16:20)

    _____

12. What was the first manifestation of the Baptism in the Holy Spirit? (Acts 19:6)

    _____

13. What was the second manifestation of the Baptism in the Holy Spirit? (Act 19:6)

    _____

14. What does a believer do when he speaks in an unknown tongue? (I Cor. 14:2,4)

    a _____

    b _____

    c _____

15. If a believer prays in an unknown tongue, what part of him is praying? (I Cor. 14:14)

    _____

16. If you pray in tongues, does your mind understand it? (I Cor. 14:14)

    _____

17. What benefit is praying in tongues or praying in the Spirit? (Rom. 8:26-27; Jude 20)

    a _____

    b _____

    This sign of tongues is given to all believers who are baptized in the Spirit. It is a personal prayer language between the believer and God.

18. What was Paul's attitude toward speaking with tongues? (I Cor. 14:5, 18)

    _____

19. Even though tongues remains of great benefit to the individual believer and is essential in prayer, what gift is best for edifying the church? (I Cor. 14:4)

    _____

20. When prophecy is given, what happens to an unbeliever who may be present? (I Cor. 14:24-25)

    a _____

    b _____

    c _____

    d _____

    e _____

21. What is the spirit of prophecy? (Rev. 19:10)

    _____

22. What are three other gifts that can be used to instruct the church? (I Cor. 14:6)

a _____

b _____

c _____

23. What is equal to prophecy? (I Cor. 14:5)

_____

24. When we assemble together, what should we bring? (I Cor. 14:26)

a _____

b _____

c _____

d _____

25. Besides praying in the Spirit, what else can we do? (I Cor. 14:15)

_____

26. What are three distinct functions of the Holy Spirit in the church? (I Cor. 12:4-6)

a _____

b _____

c _____

27. What are nine basic gifts resident in the Holy Spirit that are available to us? (I Cor. 12:8-10)

a _____   f _____

b _____   g _____

c _____   h _____

d _____   i _____

e _____

28. Beside each scripture below, list the gifts that were operating by the Spirit in the lives of the believers in the book of Acts.

a (Acts 3:1-10) _____

b (Acts 5:1-6) _____

c (Acts 9:33-35) _____

d (Acts 16:16-18) _____

e (Acts 21:10-11) _____

f (Acts 2:4-11) _____

29. When Jesus, who operated under the power of the Spirit, gave an answer concerning the woman caught in adultery, what gift was in operation? (John 8:3-11)

_____

All nine gifts are available to believers as they have need. If a demon needs to be cast out, the gift of prophecy is not needed. If a person needs to be healed, the interpretation of tongues is not needed. The Spirit manifests the different gifts as the need arises. These spiritual gifts generally operate in pairs or groups.

30. What are some of the varieties of ministries given to the church by the Holy Spirit? (Eph. 4:11; I Cor. 12:28)

a _____   f _____

b _____   g _____

c _____   h _____

d _____   i _____

e _____   j _____

These are a few of the ministries that are given by the Holy Spirit to the church. Not every one is a prophet or an apostle. Not every one has the ministry of tongues. The body of Christ would be useless if every one was an eye or every one was a mouth. Therefore, God has given each member in the body a separate ministry, function and ability. Each is given a special anointing or office. The gifts, resident in the Holy Spirit, equip each person with the ability to function in the office that God has given him.

31. What are some of the varieties of effects given to the church by the Holy Spirit? (Rom. 12:7-8, 13)

a _____   e _____
b _____   f _____
c _____   g _____
d _____

These are but a few of the different effects that God establishes in His body. The body of Christ is like a many faceted diamond with each member reflecting some aspect of the beauty and character of the Lord.

32. What are the nine fruits of the Holy Spirit? (Gal. 5:22-23)

a _____   f _____
b _____   g _____
c _____   h _____
d _____   i _____
e _____

33. Should a Christian have spiritual gifts without fruit? (I Cor. 13:1-2)

_____

34. Should a Christian have spiritual fruit without gifts? (I Cor. 12:31; I Cor. 14:1)

_____

35. What are three ways that the Spirit of God will minister to believers in the last days? (Acts 2:17)

a _____
b _____
c _____

36. For what are the manifestations of the Spirit given? (I Cor. 12:7)

_____

37. What did Jesus say about those who had received the gift of the Holy Spirit? (John 4:14; John 7:38-39)

_____

_____

MEMORY VERSE: John 4:10, 14

_____

_____

_____

_____

THE AUTHORITY OF GOD'S WORD

1. How were the Scriptures originally given? (II Tim. 3:16; II Peter 1:20-21)

    a _____

    b _____

2. What profit are the Scriptures to the believer? (II Tim. 3:16)

    a _____

    b _____

    c _____

    d _____

3. As newborn babes, having committed ourselves to the Lordship of Jesus the Messiah, what are we exhorted to do? (I Peter 2:2; II Tim. 2:15)

    a _____

    b _____

4. As we drink the milk of the Word, what will happen? (I Peter 2:2)

    _____

5. What name is given to Jesus? (John 1:1)

    _____

In submitting to the Lordship of Jesus we must also submit to the absolute authority of the written Word of God. God's written Word is God's thoughts, opinions, ideas and personality. God's Word is His expressed will to man.

6. What did Jesus say about this? (Luke 6:46)

    _____

No matter what our opinions, objections, or reasonings might be they must be brought into submission to God's Word. God's Word is the absolute and final authority over our life.

7. In light of this what must we do with any reasonings, imaginations, or any thought that would exalt itself above God's Word? (II Cor. 10:5)

    _____

    _____

8. What did Jesus say was the spiritual "food" of the believer? (Matt. 4:4)

    _____

9. What has the god of this world done? (II Cor. 4:4)

    _____

After coming out from a world filled with carnality and sin, we find that our minds have been warped and molded by sin and the things of this world.

10. How is our mind transformed? (Rom. 12:2; Eph. 5:26-27)

    _____

11. As a result of the washing of the water of the Word, what will we be? (Eph. 5:27; II Cor. 3:18)

    a _____

    b _____

    c _____

12. What can exclude us from the life of God? (Eph. 4:17-18)

_____

13. Why do God's people perish? (Hosea 4:6)

_____

14. What will happen if we reject the knowledge of God's Word and forget His law? (Hosea 4:6)

_____

From these scriptures we see that for lack of knowledge the people perish. It is Satan's will to keep men blinded to the Word of God and to the life and light that is in it. Ignorance of it can exclude us from the life of God and consequently keep us bound to sin, darkness, misery and the power of the wicked one. Consequently, the Bible is God's greatest gift to mankind. From its pages God Himself directs us in the way we should go, imparting to us wisdom and understanding that we may no longer be slaves of the evil one but sons of God who share the inheritance of the saints in light.

15. What does the Psalmist David say about the guidance that comes from God's Word? (Ps. 119:105)

_____

16. What does David say about the wisdom that comes from God's Word? (Ps. 119:98-100)
    a _____
    b _____
    c _____

17. How can young believers keep their way pure and free from sin? (Ps. 119:9-11)

_____

18. What two other things does meditation in the Word do for you? (Ps. 119:45-46)
    a _____
    b _____

19. Describe David's love for God's Word. (Ps. 119:103)

_____

20. When Jeremiah fed on God's Word, what did it become to him? (Jer. 15:16)

_____

21. How much did Job esteem God's Words? (Job. 23:12)

_____

22. As we trust in God's Word, what assurance do we have? (Ps. 119:89, 160; Num. 23:19; Matt. 24:35)
    a _____
    b _____
    c _____
    d _____

23. How can you obtain life and health to your body through God's Word? (Prov. 4:20-22)
    a _____
    b _____
    c _____
    d _____

This, in essence, is the definition of *meditation* upon God's Word. Meditation is more than a casual reading of the Scriptures. It is a diligent seeking of the revelation of it from the Lord Himself.

24. What is the outcome of the man who *meditates* in God's Word day and night? (Ps. 1:1-3)

    a _____

    b _____

    c _____

    d _____

25. What conditions did the Lord set for Joshua in order that he might be successful and inherit the promised land? (Josh. 1:8)

    a _____

    b _____

    c _____

26. What orders did the Israelites have concerning the Word of God? (Deut. 11:18-21)

    a _____   d _____

    b _____   e _____

    c _____   f _____

27. In doing this and loving the Lord with all their heart and walking in His ways, what would be the results? (Deut. 11:21-25)

    a _____

    b _____

    c _____

    d _____

28. In the spiritual armor of the Christian, what is the Word called? (Eph. 6:17)

    _____

29. Give a description of this "sword." (Heb. 4:12-13)

    a _____

    b _____

    c _____

    d _____

As we dwell in the Word of God, its edge cuts away from our lives all things that are offensive and evil. The Word in our mouths pierces the hearts of those who hear us and brings conviction of sin.

30. How did Jesus answer the devil when He was tempted? (Matt. 4:4, 7, 10)

    _____

31. How can you prove your love to Jesus? (John 14:23)

    _____

32. Describe the wise man and his house. (Matt. 7:24-25)

    _____

    _____

33. Describe the foolish man and his house. (Matt. 7:26-27)

    _____

    _____

34. Whom did Jesus call His mother and His brothers? (Luke 8:21)

    _____

35. Write down four things that result in the life of a believer who hears the Word of God and does it. (Acts 20:32; II Peter 1:4)

a _____

b _____

c _____

d _____

MEMORY VERSE: Hebrews 4:12-13

_____

_____

_____

_____

_____

_____

_____

_____

_____

—NOTES—

PRAISE, WORSHIP, AND PRAYER

1. What is the Lord worthy to receive? (II Sam. 22:4)

   _____

2. For what has God, who has called us to be His people, formed us? (Isa. 43:21)

   _____

3. How often should we praise the Lord? (Ps. 34:1-3)

   _____

4. Who should praise the Lord? (Ps. 150:6)

   _____

5. How can we honor the Lord? (Ps. 50:23)

   _____

6. What are three ways to praise the Lord? (Ps. 47:1; Ps. 98:4)

   a _____

   b _____

   c _____

7. What type of instruments were used in praising the Lord? (Ps. 150:3-5)

   a _____   e _____

   b _____   f _____

   c _____   g _____

   d _____

8. In what two other ways can we praise the Lord? (Ps. 149:1-3)

   a _____

   b _____

9. What is to be found in the mouth of the godly ones? (Ps. 149:6)

   _____

10. What power is there in praise when it is coupled with the two-edged sword, which is the Word of God? (Ps. 149:8-9)

    _____

11. When Jehoshaphat went out to battle, he sent forth the praisers before the armies of Israel. What happened? (II Chr. 20:17-23)

    _____

12. What actually happens when we begin to praise the Lord? (Ps. 22:3)

    _____

13. In the last days what is God going to restore? (Acts 15:16-18)

    _____

14. Where is the tabernacle of God to be? (Rev. 21:3)

    _____

God is raising up in these days a people in whom He can tabernacle so that all mankind might seek the Lord. We are all being built together as a dwelling of God in the Spirit.

15. What was the one thing that characterized the "tabernacle of David"? (I Chr. 15:16, 22, 24; I Chr. 16:4-6, 37-42)

_____

God Himself was enthroned upon these praises. Again in these last days, God is raising up the "fallen tabernacle of David" in the Spirit. This tabernacle is noticed because of the praise, thanksgiving, music and songs that go forth in the worship of the Lord. It is in this tabernacle that His Spirit will dwell.

16. What kind of people is God seeking? (John 4:23-24)

_____

17. How should we worship the Lord? (Ps. 2:11)

_____

18. What is one way to show this reverence? (Ps. 5:7)

_____

19. When the king had ordered the Levites to praise and worship the Lord, how did they do it? (II Chr. 29:30)

a _____

b _____

20. In what should we worship the Lord? (I Chr. 16:29)

_____

This is referring to the quality of "holiness." We are to worship the Lord in the "beauty of holiness."

21. What three things did Jesus tell His disciples about prayer? (John 16:24)

a _____

b _____

c _____

22. What did Jesus say for us not to do when we pray? (Matt. 6:7)

_____

23. Why do they use meaningless repetitions? (Matt. 6:7)

_____

24. What does your Father know? (Matt. 6:8)

_____

25. When we stand praying, what must we do if we expect to receive forgiveness from God? (Mark 11:25)

_____

26. When we pray and ask for something, what should we believe? (Mark 11:24)

_____

27. As a result, what will happen? (Mark 11:24)

_____

28. What are two reasons that a person does not receive things from God? (James 4:2-3)

a _____

b _____

29. What type of person does God hear? (John 9:31)

a _____

b _____

30. When the answer to a prayer seems to be slow in coming, what does Jesus tell us that we ought to do? (Luke 18:1)

_____

31. Jesus gave a parable about a widow and an unrighteous judge. What happened? (Luke 18:2-5)

_____

32. What did Jesus say about God in comparison to this unrighteous judge? (Luke 18:6-8)

_____

_____

33. Therefore, what should we have? (Luke 18:8)

_____

34. What promise does Jesus give us? (Matt. 7:7-8)

a _____

b _____

c _____

35. What will the Father give? (Matt. 7:11)

_____

Notice that *we* must do the asking, the seeking and the knocking.

36. In what does the Lord delight? (Prov. 15:8)

_____

37. What does the Lord hate? (Prov. 15:8)

_____

38. What privilege do those who abide in Jesus and allow His words to dwell in them have? (John 15:7)

_____

39. What three things other than what we have discussed so far can hinder our prayers? (Ps. 66:18; James 1:6-7; I Peter 3:7)

a _____

b _____

c _____

40. What should a Christian do instead of worrying? (Phil. 4:6)

_____

_____

41. How should we begin each day? (Ps. 5:3)

_____

42. What gives us the privilege of entering the holy presence of God? (Heb. 10:19)

_____

43. What does the Spirit of the Lord help us do in regard to our prayers? (Rom. 8:26-27)

_____

44. When we are trying to overcome satanic forces, what must we sometimes join with prayer? (Mark 9:29)

_____

45. What does Jesus promise will happen if two or more agree on anything for which they are praying? (Matt. 18:19)

_____

46. Whom should we pray for especially? (I Tim. 2:2)

_____

47. Why should we pray for these people? (I Tim. 2:2)

a _____

_____

b _____

_____

48. How should we pray, and what should we avoid? (I Tim. 2:8)

a _____

b _____

49. How often should we pray? (Eph. 6:18; I Thes. 5:17)

_____

MEMORY VERSE: Phil. 4:6-7

_____

_____

_____

_____

_____

_____

—NOTES—

GOD'S PROVISION FOR HEALING

1. Why did pain, sickness and death first come to man? (Gen. 3:16-19)

_____

By turning away from God in disobedience, man lost the blessing and protection of God and came under a curse and the power of the devil.

2. Who oppresses men with sickness? (Acts 10:38; Luke 13:11, 16)

_____

3. What was God's promise under the Old Covenant for those who obeyed Him? (Ex. 15:26)

_____

4. In Isaiah 53, we find a prophecy about the Messiah. What did Isaiah prophesy that Jesus would do through His atoning death in regard to physical healing? (Isa. 53:4-5)

_____

5. What does the apostle Peter say about this provision for healing? (I Peter 2:24)

_____

6. For what purpose was Jesus manifested? (I John 3:8)

_____

7. What does God promise to do for those who serve Him? (Ex. 23:25)
   a _____
   b _____

8. What did David say that the Lord did for him? (Ps. 103:3)
   a _____
   b _____

9. How many of God's promises may we claim through faith in Jesus? (II Cor. 1:19-20)

_____

10. For whom is sickness? (Deut. 7:15)

_____

11. Upon whom else will sickness come? (Deut. 28:58-59)

_____

12. What kind of sickness will come upon those who disobey God's Word and refuse to fear Him? (Deut. 28:58-61)
   a _____
   b _____
   c _____
   d _____

Those who turn from following the Lord put themselves under the Lordship of Satan. Therefore, they are at the mercy of the enemy of their souls and out from under God's protective covering.

13. What does God desire for us? (Deut. 30:19)

_____

14. What are the conditions for receiving the blessing rather than the curse? (Deut. 30:20)

a _____

b _____

c _____

15. What promise do those who trust in the Lord and make Him their refuge have? (Ps. 91:9-10)

a _____

b _____

16. What does God promise for those who return to Him from a life of sin and disobedience? (Jer. 33:6)

a _____

b _____

Consequently, we see that as men turn from sin to serve the living God, God desires not only to save man from sin but also from sickness. Jesus came to redeem man completely from the hand of the enemy.

17. For what purpose was Jesus anointed with the Holy Spirit? (Acts 10:38)

_____

18. How many did Jesus heal of those who came to Him? (Matt. 8:16; Matt. 12:15; Matt. 14:35-36)

_____

19. How many kinds of sicknesses did Jesus heal? (Matt. 4:23-24; Matt. 9:35)

_____

20. When Jesus did not heal many people, what was the reason? (Matt. 13:58; Mark 6:5-6)

_____

21. In two accounts of healing given in Matthew, what did both the leper and the centurion recognize about Jesus; and what did they both have? (Matt. 8:2, 8)

a _____

b _____

22. What does God send to heal us? (Ps. 107:20)

_____

23. The centurion demonstrated this principle. What did he say to Jesus? (Matt. 8:8-9)

_____

24. What did Jesus say about the centurion, and what did this man receive? (Matt. 8:10, 13)

a _____

b _____

25. What did Jesus look for in those who came to Him for healing? (Matt. 9:28-29; Mark 2:5; Mark 9:23)

_____

It is this simple child-like faith of accepting God's Word as truth that moves the heart of God.

26. How did Peter explain the healing of the lame man? (Acts 3:16)

_____

27. This action on Peter's part was in accordance with what command of Jesus? (Matt. 10:8)

a _____

b _____

c _____

d _____

28. What did Jesus say a person who believed in Him would be able to do? (John 14:12)

a _____

b _____

29. In what name are the sick healed and what is one method of healing? (Mark 16:18)

a _____

b _____

30. Will these people be healed? (Mark 16:18)

_____

31. What are the elders of the church to do for a sick Christian? (James 5:14)

a _____

b _____

32. What will the Lord do? (James 5:15)

a _____

b _____

33. What kind of prayer will heal the sick? (James 5:15)

_____

34. What could be one reason that this Christian was sick? (James 5:15)

_____

35. What did David say happened to him when he hid his iniquity and did not confess his sin? (Ps. 32:3-5)

_____

36. What type of man was King Hezekiah? (II Kings 20:1-3)

_____

_____

37. When Hezekiah prayed to the Lord for healing what happened? (II Kings 20:5-6)

_____

38. What type of man was King Asa? (II Chr. 15:16-17; II Chr. 16:7-10)

_____

_____

39. Because Asa had not trusted in God and had imprisoned God's prophet, what happened? (II Chr. 16:12)

_____

40. What did Asa fail to do, and as a result what happened? (II Chr. 16:12-13)

_____

41. Why are some Christians not healed? (James 4:2b)

_____

42. What was one thing that all those who desired healing from Jesus did? (Mark 10:46-50; Matt. 9:27)

_____

43. Therefore, what does Jesus exhort us to do? (John 16:24; Matt. 21:22)

_____

44. The fourth chapter of Malachi speaks of the last days. What will be prevalent among those who fear God's name? (Mal. 4:2)

_____

MEMORY VERSES: Isa. 53:5; Matt. 8:17

_____

_____

_____

_____

_____

_____

_____

—NOTES—

GOD'S PLAN FOR INNER HEALING AND DELIVERANCE

1. In what condition do most people come to the Lord? (Isa. 1:5-6; Ps. 38:3-8, 18)

_____

_____

_____

_____

_____

The Lord has not left this condition of those who come to Him unanswered.

2. What does He desire to do for us? (Ps. 23:3a)

_____

    To help in understanding man, some people look at him as being made up of three basic areas: body, soul and spirit (I Thess. 5:23). The *spirit* of man deals with the spiritual realm. It is that part of man in which the Spirit of God dwells. It can be divided into three parts: intuition, conscience and fellowship. The "conscience" is the door of your spirit. It is that which tells us right from wrong, by which we feel guilt. Sin makes the conscience dull and not sensitive to the Spirit of God by searing it with a hot iron. The conscience is the door by which we open our spirits to the Spirit of God.

    The "intuition" is the knower, that by which we perceive or sense things or circumstances. The "fellowship" area of our spirit is that which is made to have fellowship with God. It is impossible to fellowship without honesty or openness.

    The *soul* of man is that which deals with the mental and emotional realm of man. It is the seat of man's personality—his intellect, his emotions and his will. It is with his mind that a person understands.

    The *body* is that part of man which deals with the physical realm. It is dominated by the five senses and is the vehicle by which we communicate to the outside world.

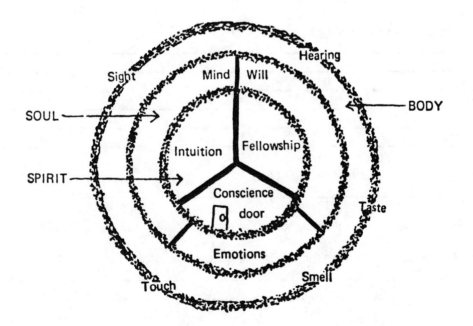

Those who come to the Lord from a life of sin are filled with brokenness, emotional scars, hurts and rejection. They are bound and imprisoned to many habits and thought patterns. Many are still full of anxiety, worry and depression. They are benumbed, badly crushed and mentally confused. When we come to the Lord, our sin of rejecting Him is forgiven. We are born again; we receive a new life and a new heart and are taken into His kingdom. However, there are many areas in our life that have been destroyed by sin. These areas are in need of restoration and transformation by the Spirit of God.

3. In fact, how does Paul say that we are transformed? (Rom. 12:2)

_____

This renewing of the mind takes place in two ways. The first is by the washing of the water of the Word through having our mind bathed and saturated in the Word of God daily. The second is by the inner healing restoration of the soul and the deliverance from anything to which the believer is held captive. God has provided a ministry for this type of renewing by the Spirit. It is found written in the book of Isaiah the prophet. It is from these Scriptures that Jesus quoted when He began His own ministry.

4. Read Isaiah 61:1-4. By what power are the ministries listed in this passage accomplished?

_____

It is these ministries listed in the Scripture quoted above that the Spirit of the Lord God is upon us to accomplish. It is for this that He has anointed us. It is in this passage that we find the basis for the ministry of inner healing and deliverance for the body of Christ. As we study this passage carefully, we find that there are three main areas involved in this ministry. They are as follows:
  1. Healing of the memories—"Binding up the broken-hearted, setting at liberty those that are bruised."
  2. Deliverance—"proclaiming deliverance to captives, the opening of prison to those who are bound."
  3. Breaking and renouncing of curses which are passed down from generation to generation—"raising up the former devastations, repairing the desolations of many generations."
  In this study, we will take each of these areas separately by going over the scriptural basis for each one. It is written in Malachi and the gospel of Matthew that before the coming of the great and terrible day of the Lord, Elijah the prophet will be sent to *restore* our hearts. *Obadiah* says, "The *deliverers* will ascend Mount Zion to judge the mountain of Esau, and the kingdom will be the Lord's." This prophetic ministry of inner healing, deliverance and restoration of the individual believer is part of the great restoration, which is taking place in the body of Christ today. It is the preparation of the Spirit for the revealing of the Lord. Before the glory of the Lord can be revealed, a "Highway of Holiness" must be prepared for Him.

5. What is the cry going forth at this hour? (Isa. 40:1-5)
  a _____
  b _____
  c _____
  d _____
  e _____
  f _____

6. What is being said to the church by the Spirit? (Isa. 57:14)

_____

It is this preparation that inner healing and deliverance brings about in the life of the believer.

7. What kind of church is Jesus coming for, and how will she be cleansed? (Eph. 5:26-27)
  a _____
  b _____

8. We see a picture of this inner working in the offering up of the burnt sacrifice. This sacrifice was not one for the atoning of sins but one offered to purify those believers who desired fellowship with God. This was not a compulsory offering but a free-will offering. It was known as the fellowship offering. What did the priests do with the "inner parts" of this offering? (Lev. 1:9)

_____

9. What does the Lord desire in the innermost parts? (Ps. 51:6-7)

_____

10. Whose responsibility is it to administer this inner healing and deliverance to the believer? (Ezk. 34:2-4)

_____

11. What does God desire to have proclaimed in the church? (Isa. 61:2)

_____

It might be noted here that "the favorable year of the Lord" is "the year of Jubilee." In this time of Jubilee in Israel, everything was returned to its rightful owner; and each man received back his inheritance. Jesus desires that the year of Jubilee be proclaimed in His church that they might receive back what the enemy has destroyed and taken from them.

12. What exortation do we have from the prophet Isaiah? (Isa. 52:1-2)
    a _____
    b _____
    c _____

I. INNER HEALING — HEALING OF THE MEMORIES

The brain has one billion cubicles for storage of information and memories. People who are mentally healthy bury unpleasantries but will go through their lives reacting to certain situations and not realizing why. Back in the mind is buried a memory that is distasteful which brings the reaction. Everyone has a reason for reacting the way he does.

1. What does the Lord desire to do for these wounds? (Isa. 1:6)

_____

2. Like what is Jesus' name? (Song of Sol. 1:3)

_____

We find that in Jesus' name abides this healing ointment.

3. If many of these hurts and bruises are hidden in our memory and forgotten, how can we know them? (Dan. 2:22)

_____

4. If we pray and ask God to reveal what is hidden there, what will He do? (Dan. 2:23)

_____

5. What gift is vital to this ministry? (I Cor. 12:8)

_____

6. The basis of this ministry is illustrated by one sentence in the Book of James. What is it? (James 5:16)

_____

_____

7. What must the attitude of the person who has been hurt be in order to receive this healing? (Eph. 4:32)

_____

8. What provision did Jesus make for this inner healing of broken hearts in the atonement? (Isa. 53:4)

_____

Any provision in the atonement must be appropriated by faith. Jesus died for the sins of the world; yet each person must individually appropriate that forgiveness by faith, or they cannot be saved. Jesus bore our sicknesses, and with His stripes we are healed. Yet, we must appropriate this healing by faith in order to be healed. Likewise, He Himself bore our griefs and carried our sorrows. The Lord has provided a ministry through which we may receive this inner healing.

9. What three things does the Lord desire His shepherds to do in the area of inner healing? (Isa. 61:1-2; Luke 4:18)

   a _____

   b _____

   c _____

10. What will the Lord give to replace the mourning? (Isa. 61:3)

   a _____

   b _____

11. What will the Lord give to replace the spirit of heaviness or fainting? (Isa. 61:3)

_____

12. What promise of this inner healing do we have from the Lord? (Isa. 57:17-19)

_____

_____

II. DELIVERANCE

1. What provision did Jesus make for deliverance on the cross? (Heb. 2:14)

_____

2. What did Jesus say to do with demons? (Mark 3:14-15)

_____

3. By what authority are demons cast out? (Mark 16:17)

_____

4. How can a person be captured by a demonic force and held in bondage? (Prov. 5:22)

_____

When a person comes to the Lord out of a life of wickedness, these cords need to be loosed so the captive can go free.

5. Why does a believer continue to remain in bondage after he has been saved? (Prov. 5:23)

_____

Because of lack of instruction and ignorance, many children of God are held in bondage. Because a person has sinned in an area so many times, he can be brought into captivity. According to this scripture, iniquities *capture* the wicked and he will be *held* with the "cords of his sins." Did not Jesus say that He came to set the *captives* free? In order to be released from this captivity, these *cords* of sin must be confessed and cleansed in the blood of Jesus.

6. What warning do we have in Isaiah? (Isa. 5:18)

_____

7. What are the "cords" by which we drag this unconfessed sin around? (Isa. 5:18)

_____

8. Why does the unrenewed mind stay corrupted? (Eph. 4:22)

_____

9. What does the Lord say about those who try to hide and conceal their transgressions? (Prov. 28:13)

_____

10. What are we exhorted to do? (Prov. 28:13)

_____

11. We see this practiced by the early church—what happened? (Acts 19:18)

_____

Therefore, we see we must be honest and truthful about the hidden things in our lives. As we confess our faults to the Lord and to those who are shepherding us, these cords will be broken; and we shall be set free from captivity. The following diagram illustrates the "cords of sin", which *hold* a person *captive to a demonic force:*

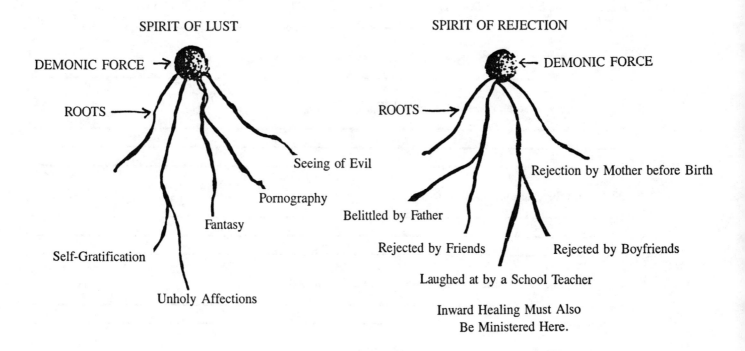

SPIRIT OF LUST

DEMONIC FORCE →

ROOTS →

Seeing of Evil

Pornography

Fantasy

Self-Gratification

Unholy Affections

SPIRIT OF REJECTION

← DEMONIC FORCE

ROOTS →

Rejection by Mother before Birth

Belittled by Father

Rejected by Friends

Rejected by Boyfriends

Laughed at by a School Teacher

Inward Healing Must Also
Be Ministered Here.

These specific sins, which have been committed, must be confessed as the Spirit of the Lord reveals them, and forsaken. For a demonic force that has its roots in hurts and wounds, each person who has inflicted hurt or pain must be forgiven from the heart of the believer. The key to this deliverance is to first get the roots out by confession and forgiveness and to then cast out the demonic spirit that is involved. If all the roots have been gotten out by the deliverance minister, there is no reason why the person will not be delivered. It is only the debris of unconfessed sin and the harboring of unforgiveness that gives the demonic spirit legal right to hold on.

12. Jesus describes this concept by means of a parable. What does Jesus say we are to do first? second? (Luke 11:20-22)

    a _____

    b _____

This "taking away" of the strong man's "armor" on which he has relied is the breaking or removing of the roots or cords of unconfessed sin.

13. What did Jesus say that the casting out of demons signifies? (Luke 11:20)

_____

14. What are three other reasons that a person can be held captive to a demonic force? (II Peter 2:19; Matt. 18:34-35; Deut. 5:9)

a _____

b _____

c _____

In many cases children, because of the sins and iniquities of their fathers, are born with a demonic hold in their life in certain areas. Children who were unwanted can be born with a spirit of rejection. Those whose parents have been involved in sexual immorality can be born with various spirits of lust. A father who has an extremely violent spirit of anger can pass it down to his children.

15. What happens to those who harbor unforgiveness? (Matt. 18:34-35)

_____

16. What must the believer do in order to get released from the "torturers"? (Matt. 18:34-35)

_____

17. If you do *not* forgive others, what will God do for you? (Matt. 6:14-15)

_____

18. As we confess these things, what happens? (Eph. 4:22-24)

a _____

b _____

c _____

19. What are three characteristics of the new self? (Eph. 4:24)

a _____

b _____

c _____

20. What two things are a sure sign of demonic activity? (James 3:14-16)

a _____

b _____

21. What else can bring demonic activity? (Heb. 12:15)

_____

All bitterness must be confessed and forsaken.

22. What are two ways that we can determine what a person is held in bondage by?
a (Heb. 4:12-13; Prov. 11:9) _____
b (Dan. 2:21-23; Ps. 13:3-4; Ps. 18:28; I Cor. 4:5) _____

As we study the Word, we discover keys that will unlock the doors of those who have been imprisoned. It is *ignorance* of the Word that can keep a man bound. Knowledge of the Word coupled with the supernatural revelation of the Spirit will bring detection of these forces.

23. What two revelation gifts of the Spirit are vital for this ministry? (I Cor. 12:8, 10)

a _____

b _____

24. What has the Spirit of the Lord anointed us for in the area of deliverance? (Isa. 61:1)

a _____

b _____

III. BREAKING OF CURSES

1. What provision did Jesus make for us in the atonement? (Gal. 3:13)

_____

2. Why did He become a curse for us? (Gal. 3:14)

_____

3. What is the "blessing of Abraham"? (Rom. 4:6-8)

a _____

b _____

c _____

When Adam sinned, the curse came upon the earth. Freedom from this curse was offered to Israel by God if they would obey Him. Final deliverance from the curse that is in the earth was provided for by Jesus through His atoning work on the cross. We, as Christians, must appropriate this provision by faith just as we do healing, forgiveness of sins, deliverance and so on.

4. What did the Lord set before Israel? (Deut. 30:15, 19)

a _____

b _____

5. Why did the Lord say the curse would come upon Israel? (Deut. 30:17-18)

_____

We see then that deliverance from this curse was only provided as Israel was faithful to God.

6. Upon whom did the Lord say that this iniquity and curse would come? (Ex. 20:5)

_____

7. What did the Lord say about those who kept His commandments? (Ex. 20:6)

_____

8. What are some other sins that God names that will bring curses upon your family? (Deut. 27:15-26; Deut. 28:45)

a _____ g _____

b _____ h _____

c _____ i _____

d _____ j _____

e _____ k _____

f _____ l _____

9. What will be the effects of these curses on future generations? (Deut. 28:46)

_____

For those who have hated God and turned from Him or sinned in the ways mentioned previously, curses have been passed down upon them, generation to generation. However, many children of God live under these curses unknowingly.

10. How are we alienated from the life of God and His blessings? (Eph. 4:17-18)

_____

Through the knowledge of the Word and the appropriation of deliverance from these curses by faith in the finished work of Jesus on the cross, the power of these curses can be broken over the lives of those who are under them. As we examine the Scriptures, we find a list of these curses given in Deuteronomy. From studying them, we can quickly discern when a person is suffering from one of them.

Study Deuteronomy 28.

11. List some of the curses of poverty. (Deut. 28:16-20, 29, 33)

a _____ f _____

b _____ g _____

c _____ h _____

d _____ i _____

e _____ j _____

12. How can you detect if a physical infirmity is a curse? (Deut. 28:27, 35, 58-61)

a _____ e _____

b _____ f _____

c _____ g _____

d _____ h _____

Notice that the majority of these illnesses are incurable.

13. What mental problems are the result of curses? (Deut. 28:28, 34, 65-67)

a _____ d _____

b _____ e _____

c _____

14. Of what curse do the following verses speak? (Deut. 28:36, 43, 49-50)

_____

15. What curse is mentioned in verse 30? (Deut. 28:30)

_____

16. What is the curse mentioned in the following verse, and what are the effects? (Deut. 23:2)

_____

_____

_____

The effects of this curse can usually be detected in those Christians who never *feel* fully accepted by the believers.

17. If you do serve the Lord but do it with complaining and murmuring, what will happen? (Deut. 28:47-48)

_____

_____

_____

By revelation of the Spirit, causes for these curses can be discerned; and the sin and effects of the curse removed from the believer and his descendants forever.

18. What reference is made to this ministry in Isaiah? (Isa. 61:4)

a _____

b _____

c _____

CONCLUSION:

19. In this aspect of inner healing, deliverance and liberation from curses, what has the Lord become to us? (Hosea 11:4)

_____

_____

20. As a result of receiving this ministry into our lives, what will be recognized about us and our descendants? (Isa. 61:9)

_____

_____

21. Having received this ministry as part of our redemption rights in Jesus, what will happen in your soul and why? (Isa. 61:10)

_____

_____

MEMORY VERSE: Isa. 61:1-2a

_____

_____

_____

_____

_____

_____

_____

—NOTES—

PRINCIPLES THAT BUILD CHARACTER

1. If you lust in your heart, of what are you guilty? (Matt. 5:28)

   _____

2. Are you to make a vow or an oath, and what is your statement to be? (Matt. 5:33-37)

   _____

3. What is anything beyond that? (Matt. 5:37)

   _____

4. What will happen to us for speaking careless words? (Matt. 12:36)

   _____

5. How shall we be justified, and how shall we be condemned? (Matt. 12:37)

   _____

6. What does the mouth speak? (Matt. 12:34-35)

   _____

7. What should your attitude be toward one who mistreats or slaps you? (Matt. 5:39)

   _____

   This is not speaking about laws for governing society, but this is speaking of personal persecution.

8. How did Jesus demonstrate this principle? (Matt. 26:51-52; Matt. 27:12; 29-30; I Peter 2:21-23)

   _____

9. What is to be your attitude when persecuted? (Matt. 5:10-12)

   _____

10. What did Jesus say our attitude toward our enemies should be? (Matt. 5:44-47)

    _____

11. How does God set this example? (Matt. 5:45)

    _____

12. Therefore, what are we to be? (Luke 6:36)

    _____

13. If you love only those who love you, is that any credit to you? (Luke 6:32)

    _____

14. If you do good only to those who do good to you, is that any credit to you? (Luke 6:33)

    _____

15. What are three attitudes that Jesus condemned, and how did He measure each offense? (Matt. 5:22) NOTE: "Raca" means empty-headed or good-for-nothing (see marginal note).

The Offense   *The Guilt*

a _____   _____

b _____   _____

c _____   _____

16. If you judge others in this way, what will happen? (Matt. 7:1-2)

_____

17. By what standard will you be judged? (Matt. 7:1-2)

_____

18. In light of this, what are we exhorted to do? (Luke 6:37)

a _____

b _____

c _____

19. If you are presenting your offering to God and remember that your *brother* has something against *you*, what are you to do? (Matt. 5:23-24)

_____

20. Of what are you to beware? (Matt. 6:1)

_____

21. What should your attitude be in giving to the Lord? (Matt. 6:4)

_____

22. If you do not forgive others, then what attitude does the Father take toward you? (Matt. 6:14-15)

_____

23. How often are you to forgive others? (Matt. 18:21-22)

_____

24. How are we to treat others? (Matt. 7:12; Luke 6:31)

_____

25. What should be your attitude toward giving to others? (Luke 6:29-30, 34-35)

a _____

b _____

c _____

26. What are we to beware of and be on guard against? (Luke 12:15)

_____

27. What did Jesus say about faithfulness? (Luke 16:10)

_____

28. What did Jesus say about unfaithfulness? (Luke 16:10)

_____

29. What attitude will God honor? (Luke 18:10-14)

_____

30. What will happen to those who try to exalt themselves? (Luke 18:14)

_____

31. What should you do if you want to be great in the kingdom? (Matt. 20:26-27)

_____

32. What example did Jesus set in this area? (Matt. 20:28)

_____

33. When invited as a guest, are you to seek the best seat for yourself? If not, then what are you to do? (Luke 14:8-11)

_____

34. When you have a luncheon or dinner, whom should you invite? (Luke 14:12-14)

_____

35. What is the greatest sign of love? (John 15:13)

_____

36. What did Jesus say for us to do if we love Him? (John 21:15-17)

_____

37. What six things are we to do for our brothers? (Matt. 25:35-40)

a _____

b _____

c _____

d _____

e _____

f _____

38. What does John exhort us to do? (I John 3:16-18)

_____

39. What are nine types of people who are blessed and find favor with God? (Matt. 5:3-11)

a _____

b _____

c _____

d _____

e _____

f _____

g _____

h _____

i _____

MEMORY VERSE: Luke 6:47-48

_____

_____

_____

_____

GOD'S PERFECT CHOICE

As we love God with all of our heart, mind, soul and strength God has promised in His Word that "no good thing will He withhold from those who walk uprightly" (Ps. 84:11b). The Bible also tells us that "He who finds a wife finds a good thing, and obtains favor from the Lord" (Prov. 18:22).

Marriage was God's idea. Marriage was God's good thing for man. When God put Adam and Eve together in the garden He pronounced that "it was good." Because marriage is God's plan, He has given us specific guidelines in His Word to help us choose a perfect mate. God has also set down in His Word certain parameters to guide single adults in their conduct toward one another.

1. What is God's plan, what is His good thing? (Gen. 2:18-25)

   _____

2. Who chose the mate for Adam? (Gen. 2:22)

   _____

Let us look at the story of Isaac and Rebekah; their story is another example of God's choosing a mate for those who serve Him. In the story of Isaac, we will consider Isaac to be an example representing all those who have been born again according to the promise. We see this reflected in Galatians 4:28, "And you brethren, like Isaac are children of promise." Abraham, a type of heavenly Father, sent his servant out to bring a wife for his son.

3. Who was the one who had chosen the wife for Isaac? (Gen. 24:12-27; esp. v. 14)

   _____

4. What type of girl was Rebekah? (Gen. 24:16)

   _____

5. God had chosen Rebekah for Isaac. What was Rebekah's attitude toward God's choice for her life? (Gen. 24:58)

   _____

6. What was Isaac doing when God brought Rebekah to him? (Gen. 24:63)

   _____

7. Did Rebekah and Isaac spend a lot of time dating and getting to know one another after God had brought them together? (Gen. 24:64-67)

   _____

8. What was Isaac's attitude toward God's choice for his life? (Gen. 24:67)

   _____

As with the story of Isaac and Rebekah, God calls us to be led by the Spirit in our male-female relationships, to walk holy and blameless before Him (I Thess. 4:1-6). Dating relationships are often based upon fleshly or worldly desires rather than upon a divine leading by the Holy Spirit. Even as we cannot obtain perfection or righteousness by the flesh (Gal. 3:3), so we cannot obtain that deep love relationship with our future mate by efforts of the flesh. Our relationships need to be Spirit-led. In Psalm 37:4 we are assured that as we delight ourselves in the Lord, *He* will give us the desires of our hearts. Instead of frantically searching for a mate through what is known as romantic dating, why not seek the Lord first and trust *Him* to bring your mate into your life? Then, led by God's Spirit, we will not satisfy the lusts of the flesh, but will instead glorify God through that one relationship which is God's "best" for us.

9. We must be careful that we do not employ worldly means to search for our life partner. What attitudes are in the world that are not from God? (I John 2:16)

   a _____

   b _____

   c _____

10. As we seek to do God's will in everything, including our choice for a mate, what assurance of stability do we have? (I John 2:17)

   _____

Relationships which are based on the lust of the flesh and of the eyes can only bring hurt. Dating relationships are too often based on these principles. We may go out with those people who are going to make us "look" good in the eyes of others or with those who appeal to our flesh. We need only to look at the results of the worldly dating system to see who the author of it is. One out of every two marriages ends in divorce. Premarital pregnancies and abortions fill our country. Most every girl and guy involved in dating usually winds up with a broken heart somewhere along the way. Lives filled with brokenness, hurt, emotional scars and rejection are what the majority of young people bring into a marriage relationship.

11. As Christians, how does God call us to conduct ourselves in our relationships with members of the opposite sex? (II Tim. 5:12; I Cor. 6:18-20; I Thess. 4:3-5)

   a _____

   b _____

   c _____

   d _____

12. With what are the unmarried to be concerned? (I Cor. 7:32; Matt. 6:32,33)

   _____

13. What are we as Christians exhorted to do? (Rom. 12:1,2; Titus 2:12-15)

   _____

From these exhortations in God's Word, it is clear that Christians are called to conduct their relationships with the opposite sex in a different way from the way the world does. We are called to be motivated by the Spirit's leading, not the lust of the flesh. We are also instructed to conduct ourselves in a pure and holy fashion, fleeing from "youthful lust." Avoid getting yourselves in situations that could stir up worldly lusts. Treat members of the opposite sex as your very own brother or sister.

The question often arises in the minds of believers, "I am afraid if I trust God to pick out my mate, he will be someone my heart does not desire—some real weird person." Since Satan always desires to present God as one who wants to give man a "raw deal," it is obvious who inspired these doubts.

14. What does the Scripture say? (Matt. 7:9-11)

   _____

15. As we trust in God for His choice for our mate, of what can we be assured? (Ps. 37:4, 5, 7; Prov. 18:22; Ps. 84:11; Prov. 19:14)

   a _____

   b _____

   c _____

   d _____

16. On what should our choice in a mate be based? (I John 2:17)

   _____

We would encourage you in the Lord to cease walking by sight and to walk by faith. Join the hundreds of young people who have seen the truth of this message and are now walking in the great liberty of spirit that this truth brings with it. The mate that God has for you will add completion to your life at every level. His choice will be that perfect one created just for you. As you commit this area of your life to Him, you will know the great blessing of being free from concern and from divided interests; as a result you will be able to give undistracted devotion to the Lord. He will bring His perfect desire to pass in your life. Remember, marriage is His idea. Those young people whom we have seen joined in this manner—not by the ways of this world but by the hand of God— have marriages built upon the Rock, upon the perfect will of God. Because these marriages are based on the will of God, they abide forever.

Therefore, we would exhort Christian young people everywhere not to seek to be conformed to this world but to dare to believe God for that perfect choice. This plan works for those who are totally commited to the Lord. Those receiving the leading of the Spirit are those seeking the Kingdom of God first, not mates, and those who are about their Father's business.

". . . I know whom I have believed and I am
convinced that He is able to guard
what I have entrusted to Him until that day."
—II Tim. 1:12

MEMORY VERSE: Ps. 37:4

_____
_____
_____
_____

—NOTES—

COMMITMENT TO THE BODY
OF THE MESSIAH JESUS

1. By what sign did Jesus say all men would know that we are His disciples? (John 13:35)

   _____

2. What kind of love did Jesus say that this is? (John 13:34)

   _____

3. In defining that love, what does the Scripture say? (I John 3:16; John 15:13)

   _____

4. This love also expresses itself in commitment to each other in the following ways:
   a (I Peter 4:8) _____
   b (Gal. 5:15) _____
   c (Phil. 2:3-4) _____
   d (I Cor. 12:26; Rom. 15:1) _____
   e (Matt. 5:44) _____
   f (James 5:16; I Cor. 12:25) _____
   g (I John 3:17-18) _____

5. What are we to be diligent to preserve? (Eph. 4:3)

   _____

As we cause division through back-biting and devouring one another, we tear down one another and destroy the work of God. This is one of Satan's main devices and tricks.

6. Why does Satan try to cause division? (Luke 11:17)

   _____

It is Satan's desire to divide and lay waste God's kingdom.

7. Therefore, if we know that any brother has anything against us, what are we to do? (Matt. 5:23-24)

   _____

8. What attitude should we have? (Eph. 4:32)

   _____

9. What are we as children of God baptized into? (I Cor. 12:13)

   _____

10. What is the body of Christ? (I Cor. 12:14)

    _____

11. Is it God's will for us to walk alone in our service for Him? (I Cor. 12:15-21)

    _____

12. Where has God placed each individual member? (I Cor. 12:18)

    _____

13. If we are like eyes seeing things in the Spirit or like ears hearing the direction in which the Spirit of God says go, can we function properly on our own? (I Cor. 12:21)

    _____

An eye sitting by itself on a table, detached from the rest of the physical body, cannot function. It is no good to itself or to anyone else apart from the physical body. It is also very ugly to look at. Yet, an eye connected to the physical body in its proper place is a great asset to the physical body because it gives light and sight to the whole body. The eye is also a very lovely thing to look at in the place where God has designed it to be. An eye apart from the body is dead and can do nothing. So it is in the spiritual body of Christ. A member of the body separate and apart from the other members cannot function. It is dead and lifeless and good for nothing. Yet, that member when attached to the rest of the body performs its function and blesses the entire body by being useful in the work of God. Each member receives its supply from the head of the body, who is Jesus.

14. Why is the manifestation of the Spirit or the gifts and operations of the Spirit given to each individual believer? (I Cor. 12:7)

_____

15. How is the body fitted and held together? (Eph. 4:16)

_____

16. In order for the joints to fit and hold the body of Christ together, in what type of "working" order must each individual part be? (Eph. 4:16)

_____

17. As each joint is supplying that which it has to give, what will happen? (Eph. 4:16)

_____

18. A beautiful parable of this corporate working of the body is found in Joel. What concept does this parable put across? (Joel 2:7-11)

_____

19. What are we, and what are we corporately being built into? (I Peter 2:5; Eph. 2:21-22)

_____

_____

20. What is Jesus building, and what type of victory will it have? (Matt. 16:18)

_____

21. For what is Jesus coming? (Eph. 5:25-27)

_____

Notice that Jesus is not coming for a superstar individual, but He is coming for a glorious church without spot or wrinkle—a church that is walking together in unity and love.

22. As your ministry develops, where has God appointed it to operate? (I Cor. 12:28)

_____

23. How is the manifold wisdom of God going to be revealed? (Eph. 3:10)

_____

24. What does Jesus call Himself? (John 15:5)

_____

25. What does He call the members of His body? (John 15:5)

_____

It is interesting to note that Jesus did not call Himself a tree, but He called Himself a vine. A tree has a main trunk with the branches directly connected and branching off from that main trunk. A vine, however, has no main trunk. It is composed of many branches connected together. In order to have a vine, you must have the branches. Each branch receives its life from the other by drinking that life-giving sap that flows from its roots. As Jesus speaks of Himself as the head and His sons as the body, so also Jesus speaks of Himself as the vine—the whole thing—and we as branches of it. Just as the head is inseparable from the body so also the branches are inseparable from the vine.

26. In order to bear fruit, what must we do? (John 15:5-6)

_____

As we have discussed the body of the Messiah, which is His church, we have found that it is not a building with a steeple on top but a living active organism. The word for the church in the Greek is "ecclesia" which means "called out ones." Those who make up a church according to the New Testament definition are true believers of Jesus, who have repented and turned from the ways of the world and of sin. As they are joined together into a local expression of Christ in the earth, they bring forth fruit.

27. Describe the church in its infancy. (Acts 2:40-47)

_____
_____
_____
_____
_____
_____

If this is the church in its infancy, how much more unity there should be in its maturity.

MEMORY VERSE: Eph. 4:11-12

_____
_____
_____
_____
_____
_____
_____
_____
_____

—NOTES—

GOD'S AUTHORITY, ORDER AND DISCIPLINE
FOR THE CHURCH

1. What types of ministries are set in the body of Christ to watch over and instruct the saints? (Eph. 4:11)

   a _____   d _____

   b _____   e _____

   c _____

2. What are their responsibilities? (Eph. 4:12)

   a _____

   b _____

3. How long will their ministries be in operation in the church? (Eph. 4:13)

   _____

   _____

4. As a result of these ministries, what will happen? (Eph. 4:14-15)

   _____

   _____

5. What office of authority has God set up in the local body? (Acts 14:21-23)

   _____

6. What are the responsibilities of the elders? (Acts 20:28; Heb. 13:17)

   a _____   c _____

   b _____   d _____

7. As watchmen of the flock of God, what specifically are the elders to do? (Ezk. 33:2-7)

   _____

8. If the watchman fails to warn the people, whose fault is it, and who is held accountable? (Ezk. 33:6-7)

   _____

9. If the people under his oversight refuse to take warning from their elder, who is responsible? (Ezk. 33:4-5)

   _____

10. In light of this, what are the members of the body exhorted to do? (Heb. 13:17; I Peter 5:5)

    a _____   b _____

11. Who is responsible for the establishing of authority? (Rom. 13:1)

    _____

12. When we resist the authority that God has set over us, what are we actually doing; and what will happen? (Rom. 13:2)

    a _____

    b _____

13. How does God define rebellion and insubordination? (I Sam. 15:23)

    a _____

    b _____

14. What should our attitude be toward those who are teaching us and leading us in the ways of God? (Heb. 13:7)

    _____

15. If we do not want to have fear of authority, what are we exhorted to do? (Rom. 13:3)

_____

16. If we do evil, what are the consequences? (Rom. 13:4)

_____

17. What did Jesus set up as the order for the correction of the rebellious and those who are out of order in the church? (Matt. 18:15-17)

a _____

b _____

c _____

d _____

18. We see this principle of church discipline practiced by the early church. What did Paul say that letting evil and sin remain in the church does? (I Cor. 5:1-6)

_____

19. What are we exhorted to do? (I Cor. 5:8)

_____

20. With whom are we *not* to associate? (I Cor. 5:10-11)

_____

21. Whom are we to judge, and whom does God judge? (I Cor. 5:12)

a _____

b _____

22. What are we to do with those "brothers" who refuse to repent of their wickedness? (I Cor. 5:13)

_____

23. The body of the Messiah is spoken of in the Scriptures as a human physical body with many parts. We see in a parable of Jesus this same teaching of removing those who will not repent, even if they are important members of the body. What did Jesus say? (Matt. 5:29-30)

_____

_____

We see this same principle practiced among the Israelites at the time of the conquest of Canaan. God had forbidden Israel to take any spoil from the city of Jericho. In Joshua chapter 7, we find that some sons of Israel acted unfaithfully to this command and took some of the things that were under the ban. Read Joshua chapter 7 before you answer the following questions.

24. What happened to the Israelites who went up against Ai? (Josh. 7:4-5)

_____

25. What reason did God give Joshua for this defeat? (Josh. 7:11-12)

_____

We find that the sin in the camp caused the whole assembly of Israel to be defeated before their enemies. So it is in the church.

26. What condition did God set before Israel for continuing to be with them? (Josh. 7:13-15)

_____

This is the same principle that is set forth in the New Testament. If sin and rebellion are allowed to remain in it, the whole body is in danger of being infected, and the church will be defeated before their enemies.

27. If we are under correction and discipline, of what is this a sign? (Heb. 12:5-8)

_____

28. Why does He discipline us? (Heb. 12:10)

   a _____ b _____

29. What kind of feeling do we have when we are under discipline? (Heb. 12:11)

_____

30. For those who have been trained by it what does discipline yield? (Heb. 12:11)

_____

31. Because of the number of Israelites, how did Moses divide the people to be governed? (Deut. 1:9-15)

_____

Paul teaches that the things that happened to the Israelites happened for our example. Their example of the governing of the people is a good one to follow. Therefore, the local body should be divided into smaller groups for more personal governing and counseling.

32. What problem had Moses run into that caused him to make this decision? (Ex. 18:13-18)

_____

_____

33. What were the qualifications for those who were chosen to shepherd, lead and judge the people? (Ex. 18:20, 21; Deut. 1:13)

   a _____ e _____
   b _____ f _____
   c _____ g _____
   d _____

34. What were their responsibilities? (Ex. 18:22)

_____

35. What disputes was Moses to judge? (Ex. 18:22, 26)

_____

36. How are these judgments supposed to be made? (Deut. 1:17; Isa. 11:3-4)

   a _____
   b _____
   c _____

37. In dividing the church for more effective counseling and discipling who should be in charge of counseling and shepherding the women? (Titus 2:3-5)

_____

The older women, under the authority of the elders, are to counsel and instruct the younger women in the ways of the Lord. Likewise, the men, under the authority of the elders, are to instruct the men in the ways of the Lord. Any cases that are too difficult or cannot be settled must be brought before the elders for judgment and further discernment.

This study covers the basic order, authority and discipline for the church. If we as a local body follow this order, we will be strong in the Lord. Each member of the body will be personally connected with other members of the body, and each member will have his needs met. The body of Christ will be a holy place where Jesus can dwell in great power and glory. The church will rise up in victory and be able to stand and conquer her enemies.

MEMORY VERSE: Heb. 13:17

—NOTES—

PROSPERITY AND GIVING

1. There are two basic principles for prosperity recorded in the Bible. In this lesson we will study both principles. One principle is found written in the book of Malachi the prophet, and the second is written in the gospel of Matthew. What are these two principles?

   a (Mal. 3:8-12) _____

   b (Matt. 6:25-33) _____

PAYING GOD WHAT BELONGS TO HIM:

2. How does a man rob God? (Mal. 3:8)

   _____

3. What is the tithe? (Neh. 10:38)

   _____

4. Besides one-tenth of our wages what else do we owe tithes on? (Lev. 27:30, 32)

   a _____   c _____

   b _____   d _____

This is what we owe God. It is not a gift. The tenth part belongs to Him. In addition to the tithe we are also commanded to give contributions.

5. How is a contribution determined? (Ex. 25:2; Ex. 35:5)

   _____

6. What happens if we fail to pay the tithe and give contributions? (Mal. 3:9)

   _____

7. Where do we put our tithe and to whom is it given? (Mal. 3:10; Neh. 10:38)

   _____

8. For what is the tithe used? (Mal. 3:10; Num. 18:21, 24)

   _____

   _____

Therefore, we see that the tithe is used to supply the need of the ministry.

9. Do the ministers pay tithes? (Num. 18:26)

   _____

10. As we give God the part of our income that belongs to Him, what will He do for us? (Mal. 3:10)

    _____

    _____

11. What will the Lord rebuke for us? (Mal. 3:11)

    _____

12. When Abraham gave God a tenth of all, what did God do for him? (Gen. 14:19-20; Gen. 24:1)

    _____

13. As we honor the Lord with our produce and with the first-fruits of our wealth, what will happen? (Prov. 3:9-10)

    _____

14. What three things did Jacob desire for the Lord to do for him? (Gen. 28:20)

a _____ c _____

b _____

15. What did Jacob promise to give God in return? (Gen. 28:22)

_____

16. How did God in turn deal with Jacob? (Gen. 33:11)

_____

17. When we give, what will be given back to us? (Luke 6:38)

_____

_____

18. In what measure or proportion will it be given back to us? (Luke 6:38)

_____

19. What is the law of sowing and reaping? (II Cor. 9:6)

_____

20. What attitude should be avoided in giving? (II Cor. 9:7)

_____

21. What kind of giver does God love? (II Cor. 9:7)

_____

22. What is God able to do? (II Cor. 9:8)

a _____

b _____

23. What will the Lord supply? (II Cor. 9:10)

a _____ b _____

Therefore, as we give bountifully, the Lord will supply us with an extra amount—not to store away and hoard—but to use and give out to meet the needs of others.

24. What are we exhorted to be on guard against? (Luke 12:15)

_____

25. Of what does life not consist? (Luke 12:15)

_____

26. What type of man was the farmer who hoarded his crops for himself, and what was his end result? (Luke 12:16-20)

_____

27. Of whom is this a parable? (Luke 12:21)

_____

28. What is a grievous evil? (Eccl. 5:13)

_____

29. What can choke out the Word? (Matt. 13:22)

_____

30. What two types of givers are there? (Luke 21:1-4)

a _____

b _____

31. Which person did Jesus say gave the most? (Luke 21:1-3)

_____

32. As riches increase, what must we be careful not to do? (Ps. 62:10)

_____

33. Where will your heart be? (Matt. 6:21)

_____

34. What are we exhorted to do? (Matt. 6:19-20)

_____

35. What is the root of all evil? (I Tim. 6:10)

_____

36. What can happen to those who desire to be rich? (I Tim. 6:9-10)

a _____

b _____

c _____

37. What will happen to the generous man? (Prov. 11:25)

_____

38. As we give bountifully, what will happen? (II Cor. 9:11-12)

a _____

b _____

c _____

39. What is giving in this way proof of? (II Cor. 9:13)

_____

SEEKING THE KINGDOM OF GOD FIRST:

40. What three things are we exhorted not to be anxious about? (Matt. 6:25)

a _____

b _____

c _____

41. Who eagerly seeks these things? (Matt. 6:32)

_____

42. If the Gentiles or unbelievers are seeking these things what should the believer be seeking? (Matt. 6:33)

_____

43. As a result, what will happen? (Matt. 6:33)

_____

44. What has God given to the person who is good in His sight? (Eccl. 2:26)

_____

45. What task has God given to the sinner? (Eccl. 2:26)

_____

_____

46. Therefore, since we have been raised up with Christ, what should we keep seeking and setting our minds on? (Col. 3:1-2)

_____

47. What kind of man was Joseph? (Gen. 39:2)

_____

48. What was the reason for Joseph's prosperity? (Gen. 39:2, 23)

_____

49. What will happen to the man who fears the Lord? (Ps. 25:12-13)

_____

50. What did Solomon ask God to give him? (II Chr. 1:7-10)

_____

51. Because Solomon did not ask for riches or wealth and was not seeking his own good but was looking to the needs of others, what did God give him? (II Chr. 1:11-12)

_____

52. What will the Lord give to those who walk uprightly? (Ps. 84:11)

_____

53. What will God give to those who fear Him and seek Him? (Ps. 34:9-10)

_____

54. Describe the man who prospers in everything that he does. (Ps. 1:1-3)

a _____

b _____

c _____

d _____

e _____

MEMORY VERSE: Luke 6:38

_____

_____

_____

_____

_____

—NOTES—

THE GREAT COMMISSION

1. When Jesus was calling His disciples to forsake all and follow Him, what promise did He give them? (Matt. 4:19)

   _____

2. What did Jesus preach? (Matt. 4:17; Mark 1:14-15)

   _____

3. What was the "Great Commission" that Jesus gave to His disciples? (Luke 24:47-48; Matt. 28:18-20)

   a _____

   b _____

   c _____

   d _____

4. What did the disciples preach? (Acts 4:2; Acts 17:18)

   _____

5. What was Paul told to do? (Acts 9:15-16; Acts 22:15)

   _____

6. What did Paul continue to do from the day that he came to know Jesus? (Acts 26:22)

   _____

7. What power has Jesus given to all those who have received the Holy Spirit? (Acts 1:8)

   _____

8. What does a wise Christian do? (Prov. 11:30)

   _____

9. What does Paul say that he did in preaching the gospel and why? (I Cor. 9:19-23) (Summarize)

   _____

   _____

10. When the Pharisees questioned the man born blind, what did he answer from his own experience? (John 9:25-33)

    _____

11. What happened as a result of his testimony? (John 9:34)

    _____

12. What will be three areas of conflict as a result of our testimony? (Matt. 10:17-18, 36)

    a _____   c _____

    b _____

13. When we are delivered up to give witness and defense for the gospel, what will happen? (Matt. 10:19)

    _____

14. Who actually will be speaking through us? (Matt. 10:20)

    _____

15. We see this happening when Stephen was questioned by the synagogue leaders. What happened? (Acts 6:10)

    _____

16. What two things should we talk about and make known to other people? (I Chr. 16:8, 9)

    a _____

    b _____

17. When people opposed Paul's testimony at Corinth, what did God tell him? (Acts 18:9)

    _____

18. What does the fear of man bring? (Prov. 29:25)

    _____

19. When some of the apostles were thrown in prison for preaching the gospel, an angel came and let them out. What did the angel tell them? (Acts 5:19-20)

    _____

20. When questioned about this, what did Peter say? (Acts 5:25-29)

    _____

21. What instruction did Paul give Timothy concerning the preaching of the gospel? (II Tim. 1:8)

    _____

    _____

22. If we confess Him before men, what will He do for us? (Matt. 10:32)

    _____

23. If we deny Him before men, what will He do to us? (Matt. 10:33)

    _____

24. Therefore, what does Jesus tell us to do? (Matt. 10:27-28)

    a _____

    b _____

    c _____

25. Why did Paul say he was free from the blood of all men at Ephesus? (Acts 20:26-27)

    _____

26. What was Paul's attitude toward his own life and the ministry that God had given him? (Acts 20:22-24)

    _____

    _____

27. What was Paul able to say before his execution? (II Tim. 4:6-8)

    a _____

    b _____

    c _____

    d _____

28. What reward is laid up for all faithful witnesses? (II Tim. 4:8)

    _____

29. What will happen to those who turn many to righteousness? (Dan. 12:3)

    _____

30. When we turn a sinner from the error of his way, what else will we be doing? (James 5:20)

    a _____

    b _____

31. What will happen to those who sow the Word of God in tears? (Ps. 126:5-6)

    a _____

    b _____

32. How did Jesus feel when He beheld the multitudes and why? (Matt. 9:36)

_____

_____

33. What did Jesus say about the harvest and the workers? (Matt. 9:37)

_____

34. For what did the Lord tell us to pray? (Matt. 9:38)

_____

35. Who are those who are blessed by God? (Isa. 32:20) (the ox and donkey represent the ministers and laborers of the gospel)

    a _____

    b _____

36. What does Jesus say to those who put off the harvesting of souls to some future date? (John 4:35)

_____

37. What does the Word say about sowing and reaping, planting and watering? (John 4:37; I Cor. 3:6-7)

_____

_____

38. How will each be rewarded? (I Cor. 3:8)

_____

39. What example did David set forth in this area? (I Sam. 30:22-24)

_____

_____

40. What are those who go out to reap sometimes entering into? (John 4:38)

_____

41. Therefore, what should he who sows and he who reaps do? (John 4:36)

_____

42. How will you overcome the enemy? (Rev. 12:11)

    a _____

    b _____

    c _____

All the apostles, except one, sealed their testimony of Jesus in their blood. Peter died upon a cross upside down. James was dragged behind a horse until his brains were dashed out upon the ground. Others were beheaded and were fed to the lions. John was exiled to a desert island to spend the rest of his life there. Yet, through these twelve men the gospel of the kingdom was preached throughout the known world. Multitudes came into the Kingdom of God. How much more should we, who have freedom to preach the gospel unhindered, go forth and preach it with all our might.

43. What should be our attitude? (II Tim. 2:3)

_____

44. What should we avoid? (II Tim. 2:4)

_____

45. Besides a soldier, what two things does Paul compare us to? (II Tim. 2:5-6)

_____

46. What should we do and why? (II Tim. 2:10)

_____

_____

MEMORY VERSE: Acts 20:24

_____

_____

_____

_____

_____

_____

_____

_____

—NOTES—

THE LAST DAYS AND THE RETURN
OF THE MESSIAH JESUS

1. When Jesus was taken up into heaven, what promise did the angels give concerning Him? (Acts 1:9-11)

   _____

2. When the Lord descends from heaven with a shout, what will happen? (I Thess. 4:16-17)

   a _____

   b _____

3. For those who are alive and remain until the coming of the Lord, what type of change will take place in them when He appears? (I Cor. 15:51-53; I Cor. 15:41-44)

   _____

4. What will this be a victory over? (I Cor. 15:54-55)

   _____

5. How long must Jesus reign in heaven before His return? (I Cor. 15:25)

   _____

We know that Jesus Himself has already gotten the victory over Satan and his host of enemies. They are already under His feet. He must reign in heaven until His body, the church, has overcome in all things through the power of the Spirit just as He Himself did.

6. What is the last enemy to be abolished? (I Cor. 15:26)

   _____

7. We have learned that the saints will receive a resurrection body when Jesus appears. What other change takes place in us meanwhile? (II Cor. 3:18)

   _____

The Greek word for "transformed" is *metamorphoō* . . .

8. Will this transformation take place in a split second of time? If not, then how will it take place? (II Cor. 3:18)

   _____

   _____

The final consummation of this transformation will take place at the return of the Lord when death is swallowed up in victory.

9. Jesus was a lamb without spot or wrinkle. What kind of church does He intend us to be? (Eph. 5:25-27)

   a _____

   b _____

   c _____

10. How will this change be accomplished in the church? (Eph. 5:26)

    _____

11. To what are we predestined? (Rom. 8:29)

    _____

12. What does it mean to be conformed to the image of Jesus? (Eph. 4:24)

    _____

13. What is said about the bride of Christ in Revelation? (Rev. 19:7)

_____

14. What is the fine linen with which she is clothed? (Rev. 19:8)

_____

Notice that before the wedding, preparation was made on the part of the bride. Likewise, as we submit ourselves to the Spirit of the Lord and the washing of the water of the Word, we too will be transformed and changed that we might be ready for His appearing.

15. What does everyone who has the "hope" of being transformed into the image of the Lord do before He returns? (I John 3:2-3)

_____

_____

16. How are we to live in this present age? (Titus 2:12)
    a _____
    b _____

17. In accordance with Jesus' high priestly prayer, what must be seen in the church by the world as a witness and testimony of Jesus? (John 17:18, 21-23)
    a _____
    b _____
    c _____
    d _____

Jesus went out before the world as a lamb without spot or wrinkle, anointed with the Holy Spirit and power, healing the sick and destroying the works of the devil. Jesus manifested the nature of God before the world. Before the end comes, Jesus will return, not for a weak defeated and sickly church, hiding out in the wilderness, but rather a victorious and holy bride, anointed with the Holy Spirit and power. The church having been washed in the water of the Word will be glorious and holy within and without. She will be going forth in the power of the Holy Spirit, healing the sick, raising the dead, casting out demons, setting the captives free. She will be a conquering church. She will be mighty and powerful in the earth as she endeavors to go forth and disciple the nations, teaching them the ways of the Lord.

18. Jesus was perfectly led by the Spirit of God. What are some of the things that characterized His life? (John 5:19-20, 30; John 12:49-50; John 12:45; John 18:38)
    a (5:19) _____
    b (5:20) _____
    c (5:30) _____
    d (5:30) _____
    e (12:49-50) _____
    f (12:45) _____
    g (18:38) _____

19. A picture of the redeemed is given in Revelation. Describe them. (Rev. 14:4)
    a _____
    b _____
    c _____
    d _____

"Not being defiled with women" means that they are not involved with the harlot system of this world. They are virgins betrothed only to Jesus. They have no other gods before them. They follow the Lamb wherever He goes!

20. What attitude does Jesus exhort us to have concerning His coming? (Luke 12:35-40)

_____

21. Jesus gives a parable about four types of servants and their rewards, at the master's return. Describe them and their rewards. (Luke 12:42-48)

Faithful Servant: _____

Reward: _____

Drunken Servant: _____

Reward: _____

Lazy Servant: _____

Reward: _____

Ignorant Servant: _____

Reward: _____

22. Jesus told another parable of 10 virgins. Five were wise and five were foolish. Who went in to the marriage feast? (Matt. 25:1-13)

_____

23. How will the day of the Lord come to the unrighteous? (I Thess. 5:2-3)

_____

24. How will the day of the Lord come to the righteous? (I Thess. 5:4-8)

_____

25. What promise do we have from the Lord? (Amos 3:7)

_____

As we continue to follow the Lord by being transformed into His image and by awaiting eagerly for the blessed hope of the glorious appearing of our Saviour, God will reveal His counsel in our midst and we will know of the things that are coming upon the earth before they happen. It is only those who are in darkness and who are ignorant of God's Word who will be overtaken suddenly. But, those who are going on to know Him will receive instruction and counsel and will be rejoicing in great anticipation of the things that are to come. They will be ready and will be put in charge of all that the Master has.

MEMORY VERSE: I John 3:2-3

_____

_____

_____

_____

_____

ANOTHER LOOK AT THE LAST DAYS

1. What will the coming of the Son of Man be like? (Matt. 24:37)

   _____

2. What were the worldly people involved in? (Matt. 24:38)

   _____

3. Who was taken away in judgment by the flood in Noah's day? (Matt. 24:39)

   _____

4. In like manner, who will be taken away in judgment at the coming of the Lord? (Matt. 24:40-42)

   _____

5. Who will be left? (Matt. 24:40-42)

   _____

6. According to Proverbs, who will remain in the land; and who will be cut off from the earth? (Prov. 2:21-22)

   a _____

   b _____

7. Who will be exterminated from the earth? (Isa. 13:9)

   _____

8. Who will inherit the earth? (Matt. 5:5)

   _____

9. In Hebrews, we read that once more God will shake the heavens and the earth. What will remain? (Heb. 12:25-27)

   _____

10. What kingdom are we a part of? (Heb. 12:28-29)

    _____

1. Hebrews also tells us that our God is a consuming fire. When He appears, who will be fearful; and who will be able to stand? (Isa. 33:14-15)

   a _____

   b _____

12. On whom will the day of the Lord come like a trap? (Luke 21:34)

    _____

    _____

13. What are we exhorted to do? (Luke 21:36)

    _____

    _____

14. For those who put their trust in Jesus, what did He pray? (John 17:15)

    _____

15. Who does Jesus exhort us to remember as an example? (Luke 17:28-32)

    _____

Lot's wife was turned into a pillar of salt, because she looked back when she was told not to. Her heart was still yearning after earthly things.

16. Jesus said what signs would occur before His coming? (Matt. 24:3-14)

a (v. 5,11) _____

b (v. 6) _____

c (v. 7) _____

d (v. 9) _____

e (v. 10) _____

f (v. 12) _____

g (v. 12) _____

h (v. 14) _____

Many of these signs have been fulfilled over the years since Jesus prophesied them. Some of them have been present in every generation. Yet, Jesus said these signs shall increase in *intensity* as "birth pangs" before the new age begins.

17. What two signs did Jesus say would mark the generation in which He will return? (Matt. 24:32-34 with Ps. 102:13; Luke 21:24)

(fig tree represents the nation of Israel in Scripture)

a _____

b _____

In 1948, Israel became a nation again for the first time since the diaspora (the scattering of the Jews to the four corners of the earth). In 1967, Israel regained Jerusalem from Gentile dominion. This was the first time she had possessed it since 70 A.D. The generation that sees this happen shall not pass away until all these things be fulfilled.

18. How long must Jesus remain in heaven before His return? (Acts 3:21)

_____

_____

As we read the prophets, we find that they speak of a two-fold restoration: the restoration of the church and the restoration of the nation of Israel. According to these prophets this restoration takes place simultaneously.

19. What two-fold picture do you see in Isaiah? (Isa. 11:10-12)

(the root of Jesse is Jesus)

a _____

b _____

21. What will the Jews say of the Lord in those days? (Jer. 23:7-8)

_____

_____

22. What covenant will the Jews become partakers of? (Jer. 31:31-34)

_____

23. What will happen when Israel returns to her Lord, and will she ever be cast out again? (Jer. 31:38-40)

_____

_____

24. What two events are recorded here? (Jer. 33:14-16)

a _____

b _____

25. What two-fold restoration is recorded by Hosea? (Hosea 2:23; Hosea 3:1-5; Rom. 9:25)

a _____

b _____

26. When will this happen? (Hosea 3:5)

_____

27. Paul speaks of this restoration. What does he say? (Rom. 11:12-27)

_____

_____

The Lord will have one new man. The believing Gentiles as well as the believing Jews will together make up the glorious body of Jesus the Messiah.

28. As the glory of God comes upon His church in the last days, what will happen in the world? (Isa. 60:1-7)

_____

29. It is recorded by the prophet Ezekiel that in the last days when Israel has returned to her land, the Lord will bring Gog (which is the nation of Russia) against them. What is God's purpose in this? (Ezk. 38:16)

_____

30. When Russia comes upon the mountains of Israel, what supernatural acts of judgment will take place? (Ezk. 38:18-22)

a _____

b _____

c _____

This will be a supernatural judgment against Russia to show forth God's glory and power to the nations.

31. When this happens, what will the nations recognize? (Ezk. 38:23; Ezk. 39:21)

_____

32. What will the house of Israel recognize from that day on? (Ezk. 39:22)

_____

33. What will the nations recognize about Israel? (Ezk. 39:23-24)

_____

_____

34. What will Israel realize? (Ezk. 39:25-28; Zech. 12:10)

_____

_____

35. What will the Lord then do for them? (Ezk. 39:29)

_____

36. We see a more detailed picture of the outpouring of the Spirit upon Israel recorded by the prophet Zechariah. In what order will the Lord save them? (Zech. 12:7-8)

_____

37. When the Lord pours His Spirit upon them, what will they recognize and mourn over? (Zech. 12:10; Zech. 13:6)

_____

_____

38. What will be opened on that day? (Zech. 13:1)

_____

39. When did Jesus say that the Jews as a nation would see Him again? (Matt. 23:37-39)

_____

Jesus quotes this passage from a portion of the "Great Hallel" in the Psalms, which is Messianic in content. He was saying that until Israel recognized Him as their Messiah and Redeemer, He would not return to Jerusalem. In the land of Israel, from the city of Jerusalem and Mount Zion, Jesus will set up His earthly reign as King for 1,000 years of peace. From His own lips, Jesus said He will not return there until the Jews personally invite Him. This is the same thing that Zechariah prophesied that they would do.

40. When Jesus returns as King, who will rule with Him? (Rev. 2:26-27; Rev. 3:21; Matt. 19:27-28)

_____

From the prophets, we have established that before the glorious return of the Lord, both Israel and the church will be restored in power and glory. When the church becomes glorious, multitudes of nations and kings will come into the Kingdom of God; and through supernatural acts of God, all of Israel will come to repentance and the knowledge of the truth. This study covers a few of the events spoken of by the prophets. These are not all the events that will take place before the Lord's return; but as we see the hand of God moving to restore His church and to recover again the nation of Israel, we can know that the end is very near, even at the door.

MEMORY VERSE: Acts 3:21

_____

_____

_____

_____

_____

_____

_____

FAITH TOWARD GOD

1. Before we can leave the elementary teaching about the Messiah and press on to maturity, what foundation must we have? (Heb. 6:1-3)

   a _____

   b _____

   c _____

   d _____

   e _____

   f _____

In order to lay this strong foundation on which we may properly build, the following studies have been prepared on the foundational truth of "Faith toward God." Without a true understanding of Biblical faith, we will find it impossible to come into that spiritual maturity that God desires to see in each one of His children. Faith makes the difference between defeat and victory in a Christian life. (Portions of the following studies on faith were inspired by the writings of Kenneth Hagin.)

Without faith, it is impossible to please God. By faith, the men of old gained approval from God. By faith, they conquered kingdoms, performed acts of righteousness, obtained promises, shut the mouths of lions, quenched the power of fire, escaped the edge of the sword, from weakness were made strong, became mighty in war and put foreign armies to flight. They were stoned, sawn in two, put to death with the sword; they were destitute, afflicted and ill-treated. All these gained approval through their faith. They believed God, and it was accounted to them as righteousness. It is our goal through these studies to build a strong foundation of faith in the believer's life so that each believer may show the same diligence as those great men of faith who went before them. As a result, the believer will not become sluggish but will be an imitator of those who through faith and patience inherit the promises and press on to maturity in God.

2. What does God demand that we have in order to please Him? (Heb. 11:6)

   _____

3. What is the relationship between faith and pleasing God? (Heb. 11:6)

   a _____

   b _____

We see then that "without faith, it is impossible to please Him . . ." Therefore, if God demands that we have faith when it is impossible for us to have faith, then we have a right to challenge His justice. But if He places within our hands the means whereby faith can be produced, then the responsibility of whether we have faith or not rests on us.

God has told us that without faith, it is impossible to please Him; but He has also told us how to get faith. If we do not have faith, it is not God's fault. To blame God for any lack of faith is ignorance, for God has provided the way whereby everyone can have faith. Let us examine a few scriptures to discover the provision for faith that God has made.

4. Through what are we saved? (Eph. 2:8)

   _____

5. How do we get faith in order to be saved? (Rom. 10:8-10, 13, 14, 17)

   _____

So then, we see that faith comes through "hearing the Word of God."

6. From studying the passage in Romans, what three steps does a person take in order to receive salvation?

   a _____

   b _____

   c _____

7. God sent an angel to the house of Cornelius as he stood praying. The angel told him to send for Simon Peter. What was Peter supposed to tell Cornelius? (Acts 11:13-14)

_____

Cornelius had not yet heard the Gospel; he was not saved. The expression "who shall tell you words by which you will be saved" shows that men are saved by hearing the Words of God. The reason for this is that "faith comes by hearing, and hearing by the Word of God."

8. In the following passage, what three things did Paul do? (Acts 14:7-10)
   a (v. 7) _____
   b (v. 9) _____
   c (v. 10) _____
   What three things did the man do?
   a (v. 9) _____
   b (v. 9) _____
   c (v. 10) _____

9. Where did the man get the faith to be healed? (Acts 14:9)

_____

10. What is faith? (Heb. 11:1)

_____

Moffatt's translation of this verse reads, "Now faith means that we are confident of what we hope for, convinced of what we do not see." Many people want to receive something from God and then believe. However, Biblical faith is believing first, then receiving the visible manifestation of it. This is the kind of faith that God has.

11. How did God form the world? (Heb. 11:3)

_____

_____

12. We see this faith of God outlined by Jesus. What principles are found in the following passage? (Mark 11:22-23)
   a _____ c _____
   b _____ d _____

13. We see this kind of faith operating in the heart of God when He created the world. What did He do?
   a _____ c _____
   b _____

14. When we pray for something, what are the conditions for receiving an answer to our prayer? (Mark 11:24)

_____

Jesus was simply saying that you have to believe it before you can receive it. Faith says "I have it even though I can't see it." We must believe it because God's Word says it, then it materializes. Stand firm on God's Word, and results will be forthcoming. If, instead, we sit around and groan, sigh, gripe and complain—waiting until we see the manifestation of the promise before we believe—we will never get very far. "For faith is . . . the evidence of things not seen."
We will now examine two types of faith:
1. Head knowledge faith—seeing is believing.
2. Heart knowledge faith—I believe it because God says it is true.

15. Why did Thomas find it hard to believe that Jesus was alive? (John 20:24-25)

_____

_____

_____

16. At what point did Thomas believe? (John 20:26-29)

_____

17. What exhortation did Jesus give him? (John 20:29)

_____

Abraham is an example of a man who did not see and yet believed. He had that heart kind of faith. Abraham was 100 years old when God gave him the promise of a son. His wife was 90—well past the years of child-bearing. He believed the promise because *God said it was true.*

18. Describe Abraham's heart faith. (Rom. 4:17-21)

a (v. 17) _____

b (v. 18) _____

c (v. 19) _____

d (v. 20) _____

e (v. 21) _____

19. According to the above passage, if Abraham did not consider physical knowledge or feelings, what did he consider? (Rom. 4:17-21)

_____

Notice that Abraham did *not consider his body.* Many people desiring healing, for example, look to their physical body for symptoms of sickness or healing. Abraham did not consider his body; he looked *only* to the promise of God.

20. How do we put our faith in God's Word? (I John 5:9)

_____

John tells us that if we receive the words of our friends as truth, how much more we should receive the Words of God. Faith is a matter of simply receiving God's Words as true. This is the most crucial and important principle of faith. "If we receive the words of men, the Words of God are greater." The following two stories demonstrate the truth of this scripture:

Mary went shopping on Monday morning. In one of the shops, she met a school friend whom she had not seen in three years. Mary asked the girl to come to her home for dinner that evening. The friend accepted. Mary did some last minute grocery shopping and spent the rest of the afternoon preparing for the visit. She did *not* worry and fret all afternoon as to whether her friend would arrive or not; she did not worry whether her friend would keep her word. Instead, she looked forward with great anticipation to the meeting that they were going to have together. At 7 o'clock everything was ready, and she was expectantly awaiting her guest with joy in her heart.

Mary *received* the witness of a friend. Her actions for the rest of the day were based upon that word.

Mary is also a Christian. She read in Matthew 6 that she should not be anxious for what she will eat or drink or for her clothing, for God knows that she needs all these things. If she would seek the Kingdom of God first and His righteousness, all these needs would be taken care of by God.

This promise seemed too good to be true. The mailman came and Mary went to the door to get her mail. She received three bills in the mail, a total of which was $300 more than she had to pay. Mary spent the rest of the day worrying and fretting about whether God would really meet her need. Was His Word to her really true? If only she could get enough faith to *make* the Word happen. She became so worried that she found her thoughts filled with the cares of this life and found it hard to think on the things of the Lord. Mary spent the rest of the day worrying about whether God would keep His Word to her. "If we receive the word of man, the Word of God is greater."

21. In light of God's Word, what should Mary have done?

_____

   From these examples, we can see that Mary naturally acted in faith toward her friend's word yet failed to act in the same kind of faith toward God's Word.
   Faith is *not* something that we try to *get* to make the Word happen. It is accepting the Word of God at face value, receiving it as we would the word of a trusted friend.

22. What promise do we have regarding the validity of God's Word? (Num. 23:19)

_____

MEMORY VERSE: I John 5:9a

_____

_____

_____

_____

—NOTES—

FAITH IS LOOKING CONTINUALLY AT THE WORD
AND BEING A DOER OF IT

Faith is not something that we have as much as it is something that we do. We have seen that faith is not hoping that we will see the answer in the future; faith is believing that we have the answer now. Faith sees the answer by continually looking into the Word and acting according to what it sees.

1. How does the kind of faith—that which contradicts circumstances and sees the answers—grow strong in your life? (Prov. 4:20-22)

   _____

   _____

To "give attention" to God's Word means to study and obey God's Word. Many Christians have failed, been defeated, are weak and sickly because they have disobeyed this basic command of God and have let the Word of God depart from before their eyes. However, if you obey this command by keeping the Word of God ever before you, then you will see yourself as more than a conqueror; and you will be without sickness and without disease. Many people pray, and instead of seeing themselves with the answer they see themselves as getting worse. Forgetting to look continually at the Word, they look at the wrong thing—at the symptoms, at conditions, at themselves—and so they walk in unbelief and destroy the effects of their prayer.

2. Abraham had a faith that contradicted circumstances. What did Abraham look at, and what did he refuse to consider? (Rom. 4:19-21)

   _____

We as children of faith and sons of Abraham must constantly stand firm upon God's Word even in the face of adverse circumstances and contradictory evidence.

3. What assurance do we have from the mouth of the Lord concerning the truth and steadfastness of His Word? (Isa. 55:11)

   _____

Faith contradicts circumstances. Faith agrees with God's Word. Real faith "says" the answer.

4. What is the evidence of what man really believes in his heart? (Rom. 10:10)

   _____

Our faith in God becomes stronger as we vocalize what is in our heart.

5. We find this principle given in the teachings of Jesus. What did He say about our confession? (Mark 11:23)

   _____

6. Did Jesus say it was enough to believe it in your heart only? (Mark 11:23)

   _____

Jesus said that "out of the abundance of the heart, the mouth speaks." What you say reveals what you believe in your heart to be true. God and His Word are inseparable. God's Word is an expression of Himself. As we grow in love and trust toward God, we must begin to say about ourselves what the Word says. We have what God says we have. We are what God says we are. If God says we are strong, then we are. If He says He cares for us, then He does. If He says we are healed, then we are.

7. How do we overcome the enemy? (Rev. 12:11)

   a _____

   b _____

   c _____

In both the Old and New Testaments, we see examples of how God's people by putting their faith into action, were able to accomplish mighty deeds. Great miracles were wrought by humble men, who in child-like faith, acted upon God's Word.

Let us now look at the examples set forth by Joshua at the battle of Jericho.

8. What did God tell Joshua? (Josh. 6:2)

_____

9. Did this mean that Joshua and the children of Israel could sit back and relax while the city automatically became theirs? (Josh. 6:3-5)

_____

10. What explicit instructions did God give them about possessing the land that He had already given them? (Josh. 6:3-5)

_____

_____

_____

_____

_____

_____

God told them exactly what to do. They had to believe that Word and *act* upon it. Their acting upon the Word was their faith in action. Notice that they were to shout while the walls were still up. Anybody can shout when the walls are down; it does not take any faith to do that. The Israelites were required to act out their faith. They "shouted" first; then they saw the result. We must be careful not to sit and wait for something to come to us. We must have an active faith and go up and possess the land that God has given us for an inheritance.

Let us look at this same faith in action in the New Testament.

11. While Jesus was teaching in a house, some men brought their friend to Him to be healed. Because they had difficulty in reaching Jesus, did they give up and go home? (Luke 5:18-19)

_____

12. What did they do? (Luke 5:18-19)

_____

Notice that they did not shrug their shoulders and go back home. They did not say, "Well, at least we tried. We did the best we could." They did not give up that easily.

13. What did Jesus "see"? (Luke 5:20)

_____

Jesus saw their *action* as a demonstration of the faith that was in their hearts.

14. How did the invalid demonstrate his faith? (Luke 5:24-25)

_____

As we act out our faith in His Word to us, we will reap the results. One of the best definitions of faith is this—believing God's Word is acting as though it is true.

The following is a formula for faith:
1. Find a promise in God's Word for whatever you are seeking.
2. Believe God's Word as you would the word from a friend.
3. Do not consider the contradictory circumstances.
4. Praise God for the answer, acting on the Word of God.

15. What are we exhorted to do? (James 1:22)

_____

16. How is faith demonstrated outwardly? (James 2:17-18)

_____

17. How did Abraham demonstrate his faith by works? (James 2:21)

_____

18. When Abraham acted on God's Word by offering up his only son, what was he demonstrating? (Heb. 11:17-19)

_____

_____

19. How did Noah demonstrate his faith by works? (Heb. 11:7)

_____

20. How is faith perfected or made more perfect? (James 2:22)

_____

It is in the "doing" of the Word that our faith is made stronger day by day. If we have seen that God has been faithful to His Word in small things, we will *not* doubt when the big things come along.

21. What is a hearer of the Word but not a doer likened to? (James 1:23-24)

_____

We, as the New Creations of God, can discover what our lives in Him are to be and what we are like as a new creature by looking into the Word as we would look into a mirror. We must be careful that we do not walk away and act like the old earthly creatures we used to be. We must be careful that we do *not* forget what God says we are, what He says we can have and what He says we can do.

22. How can we avoid this? (James 1:25)

    a _____

    b _____

    c _____

23. What kind of life will we have? (James 1:25)

_____

MEMORY VERSE: James 1:25

_____

_____

_____

_____

_____

_____

_____

_____

THE CONFESSION OF GOD'S WORD BUILDS FAITH
AND FIXES THE LANDMARKS OF YOUR LIFE

Confession is faith's way of expressing itself. Faith's confession creates reality. It is always possible to discover a person's belief by what he says. According to Jesus, "Out of the abundance of the heart, the mouth speaks." If a man's confession is wrong, his believing is wrong. If his believing is wrong, his thinking is wrong. If his thinking is wrong, it is because his mind has not been renewed by the Word of God. All three—believing, thinking and saying—go together. God has given us His Word to get our thinking straightened out.

Confession, then, is affirming something we believe. It is testifying to something we know. It is witnessing for a truth we have embraced.

1. In what way is the Word to be given to the lost? (Mark 16:15)

_____

It is through our confession or preaching of the Word that the world hears the Gospel. If we do not carry the Word to the world, then we waste our time praying for God to do something. If we could just pray and get people saved, we would not need to send missionaries all over the world. In obedience to Jesus' command, the disciples went forth preaching the Word everywhere.

2. As the disciples went forth and preached the Word, what did the Lord do for them? (Mark 16:20)

_____

God did not do anything until the disciples preached the Word; then the signs followed. Notice also that the signs did not follow an individual but followed the preaching of the Word.

There is no faith without confession. Paul wrote, "And how shall they believe in Him Whom they have not heard. And how shall they hear without a preacher [a confessor]?" Likewise, in our daily lives and conversation, confession is faith's way of expressing itself. Faith, like love, is of the heart and of the spirit. We know that there is no love without word or action. We cannot reason love into people, nor can we reason love out of them. It is of the heart. There is no faith without confession. The confession of the believer fixes the landmarks of his life.

3. What did Jesus say about our confession? (Mark 11:23)

_____

According to the words of Jesus, if we believe what we say, it will come to pass—whether it be success or failure, sickness or health, weakness or strength. The reason the majority of Christians are weak is that they never dared to make a confession of who they are in Christ. The confession of a believer fixes the landmarks of his life. In the Old Testament, we find this truth illustrated in the lives of the twelve Israelites who were sent to spy out the land.

4. What confession of faith did 10 of the spies make? (Num. 13:25-33)

_____

5. What confession of faith did Caleb and Joshua make? (Num. 13:30; Num. 14:6-10)

_____

_____

6. What landmark did the 10 spies fix in their lives because of their negative confession? (Num. 14:36-37)

_____

7 What landmark did the congregation of Israel fix in their lives through all their grumbling and complaining? (Num. 14:27-29)

_____

8. What landmark did the fathers fix in the lives of their children? (Num. 14:31-33)

_____

_____

_____

9. What landmark did Joshua fix in his life through his confession? (Num. 14:38; Josh. 1:1-8)

_____

_____

10. What landmark did Caleb fix in his life through his confession? (Num. 14:24; Josh. 14:6-14)

_____

_____

11. What is in the power of the tongue and with what will a man be filled? (Prov. 18:20-21)

_____

_____

12. What are we exhorted to do as believers in light of Israel's failure? (Heb. 3:16-19; Heb. 4:1-2)

_____

13. Why did the Word of God not profit them? (Heb. 4:2)

_____

The Amplified Version of this verse reads: ". . . but the message they heard did not benefit them, because it was not mixed with faith (that is, with the leaning of the entire personality on God in absolute trust and confidence in His power, wisdom and goodness) by those who heard it."

If we find ourselves at the bottom of life's ladder, it is because that is all we have believed for. There is a Godward side and a manward side to every battle, every victory, and everything that we receive from God. We have our part to play. If there is any failure, it has to be on our part. God is not going to fail. If we see to it that we do our part, then we can be sure that there will be an answer and a victory.

14. A certain woman who had been sick for twelve years came to Jesus for healing. What is the first thing that this woman did? (Mark 5:25-34)

_____

So we see that the first thing the woman did was to say what she believed. She could have made a negative confession instead of a positive one. She could have said that it was no use and that it was best for her to die. But she spoke positively. If we are defeated, we are defeated with our own lips.

15. What is the second thing the woman did? (Mark 5:27)

_____

Our actions either defeat us or they cause us to overcome. According to our actions, we either receive or are kept from receiving. The woman acted out her faith.

16. What is the third thing she did? (Mark 5:29)

_____

Notice that the feeling and the healing followed the saying and the acting. Many people fail to receive because they want the feeling and the healing before they are willing to say it and do it.

17. What is the fourth thing the woman did? (Mark 5:33)

_____

Jesus also desires for us to tell others that they, too, might receive from Him.

We see these four steps also demonstrated in the life of David as he fixed the landmark of his life and possessed the confession of his mouth.

18. What was the first thing David did when he went to fight Goliath? (I Sam. 17:45-47)

_____

David had faith, not in his own strength, but in God's power and might. He was not trusting in himself. He was trusting in the Lord. He *confessed* what he believed in his heart.

19. What is the second thing that David did? (I Sam. 17:49)

_____

David *acted* upon his faith. If David had been led by his natural senses, if he had listened to human reasoning, he would have known that it would be impossible to kill a giant with a shepherd's sling. He was tuned to the inner voice of faith, not to the outer voice of human reasoning.

20. What was the third thing David did? (I Sam. 17:50)

_____

David *received* the victory for the Israelites over their enemies, the Philistines.

21. What is the fourth thing that David did? (I Sam. 17:54)

_____

David *published* the news of victory throughout the land.

We must first, *say* what we believe to be true;
second, *act* on what we believe to be true;
third, *receive* what we believe to be true;
fourth, *tell* others what we received from God that they too might believe.

In doing this we can fix the landmarks of our lives for good and win victories for the Kingdom of God, ourselves and our brothers and sisters in the Lord. Out of weakness we will be made strong and will be able to put to flight the armies of the evil one.

MEMORY VERSE: Mark 11:23

_____
_____
_____
_____
_____
_____
_____
_____
_____
_____

"THE BOLD CONFESSORS OF THEIR FAITH"

Very few Christians actually realize the place that confession holds in God's scheme of things. Unfortunately, whenever the word "confession" is used, many invariably think of confessing sins, weaknesses and failures. That is the negative side of confession. There is, however, a positive side of confession, which the Bible has *more* to say about than the negative. Webster's dictionary defines "confession" not only as a confession of sins, but as a "statement of one's beliefs; especially those of the Christian faith." That is why true Christianity throughout the centuries has been known as "The Great Confession." Webster's dictionary also defines a "confessor" as "a Christian who has suffered for his *faith*". The apostles and early fathers of the faith were "bold confessors" of the Word of God. Let us look at five of these "bold confessors."

1. We find the first three denying the King's order to bow down before the golden image. What was the "bold confession" of Shadrach, Meshach, and Abed-nego? (Dan. 3:16-18)

_____

_____

2. As a result of the "bold confessions" of their faith, what happened? (Dan. 3:21)

_____

3. Because of their faith and commitment to God, loving not their lives unto death, what did the Lord do for them? (Dan. 3:24-27)

_____

4. What did the King say about their "bold confession" of faith? (Dan. 3:28)

a _____

b _____

c _____

As a result of these men's "bold confessions" of faith, God was exalted and glorified; and according to the Scripture, they prospered greatly in the province of Babylon.

5. We find the next man denying the edict of the King, which said that anyone making a petition to any god or man besides the King, was to be thrown to the lions. What was Daniel's "bold confession"? (Dan. 6:10)

_____

_____

6. As a result of the "bold confession" of his faith, what happened? (Dan. 6:16-17)

_____

7. Because of Daniel's faith and commitment to God, loving not his life unto death, what did the Lord do for him? (Dan. 6:20-23)

_____

8. Because of the "bold confession" of Daniel's faith, what was recognized about his God? (Dan. 6:25-27)

a _____

b _____

c _____

d _____

So God was glorified and exalted through the faith of Daniel and as it is written in verse 28: "Daniel enjoyed success in the reign of Darius and in the reign of Cyrus the Persian."

9. We find the fifth "bold confessor" of faith boldly proclaiming and confessing the Word of God before the high priest and elders of Israel and the synagogue of the Freedmen. What was the "bold confession" of Stephen? (Acts 7:51-52, 55-56)

_____

_____

_____

_____

10. As a result of the "bold confessions" of Stephen's faith, what happened? (Acts 7:57-60)

_____

11. Because of Stephen's faith and commitment to God, loving not his life unto death, what happened? (Acts 7:58, 60; Acts 9:15)

_____

_____

As a result of Stephen's "bold confession" and his forgiving spirit, a young man named Saul, who was later to become the great Apostle Paul, heard the gospel and was released from his sin of murdering Stephen that he might be saved.

12. What blessing did Stephen's interceding for his murderers and his bold confession bring to the world? (Acts 9:11-16)

_____

13. What does Paul record in Hebrews about the "bold confessions of the faith"? (Heb. 11:33-38)

_____

_____

We see that by faith great victories were won for the Kingdom of God, and also by faith men were willing to give their lives for what they believed to be true. This kind of faith is the very essence and heart of the gospel. It is the kind of faith that agrees with God's Word and stands for it; never backs down, even in the face of death. By this faith, the men of old gained approval from God. This is faith in its maturity.

14. How shall we overcome the enemy? (Rev. 12:11)

a _____

b _____

c _____

MEMORY VERSE: Rev. 12:11

_____

_____

_____

_____

_____

_____

GOD'S PREDETERMINED PURPOSE
VERSUS
MAN'S FREE WILL

Is everything that happens God's direct will? Is God's will always done? Human beings cannot thwart God's ultimate plan for the world; but they can and do thwart His plans that they, as individuals, should have a part in. Men cannot prevent God's ultimate plan achieving its end. The Kingdom of God will come upon the earth as it is in heaven, and the glory of the Lord will fill the earth whether they want it to or not. In this sense, we may well cry "Hallelujah, the Lord our God, the Almighty reigns." But what men can do is personally drop out of this Kingdom or from their appointed places in it. God ordains that the Kingdoms of this world shall become the Kingdoms of our God and of His Christ; however, He does not ordain which particular individuals will accept His plan for them in His Kingdom.

1. What is recorded in Isaiah concerning God's predetermined purpose in the earth? (Isa. 46:10-11)

    _____

2. As individuals, how did the Pharisees and lawyers respond to God's purpose for them? (Luke 7:30)

    _____

Even though God's plans for the universe certainly succeed, an individual may still reject God's plan for his part in it. The reason for this is that God does not want mule-like servants who have to be forced to obey Him all the time. He wants those who will freely accept His instruction and counsel. As a man or woman desires for his marriage partner to want his companionship out of love and free-will, not out of obligation; so also God wants relationships with His creation based on mutual affection and love, not relationships based on "force." God desires for all men to repent and enter a free love-relationship with Him. But, if He "forced" men to repent, then their allegiance would not be freely given. Therefore, God leaves man with a free choice. He does not "force" a man to repent who chooses a path that does not delight Him.

Let us now search the Scriptures to discover more about man's responsibility and his free will to defy the will of God or to follow that will.

3. In the story of God choosing a wife for Isaac, what was God's plan; and what part did the woman have in that plan? (Gen. 24:7-8)

    a _____

    b _____

4. What was the woman's choice? (Gen. 24:57-58)

    _____

5. Judas was also called by God. For what was Judas called, and what was his choice? (Acts 1:24-25)

    a _____

    b _____

The office, the calling and the task to fulfill for Rebekah and Judas were ordained by God alone. What God did not ordain was how they would match up to the task He had given them. Rebekah, through the act of her will, chose to fulfill her calling through the power of the Spirit. Judas did not. It was his own choice. It was not that he could somehow "unchoose" or "uncall" himself—for both calling and election were Jesus' decision. What Judas could and did do was to fall away from the ministry he had been given and so forfeit the blessing he could have brought and enjoyed.

6. As a result of Rebekah's choice, what blessing did she receive? (Gen. 24:60)

    _____

7. The Lord established this principle of free will very early in Israel's history as a nation. What choice was set before Israel? (Deut. 30:11-20)

_____

8. What was God's desire for them? (Deut. 30:19-20)

_____

9. Was this commandment too difficult for them or impossible for them to follow? (Deut. 30:11-14)

_____

God set this principle of free will before Israel in its early life as a nation. We will now look into the Scriptures to see this principle set before them by God again and again, and we will see how Israel responded.

10. What did Israel desire for Samuel to do for them? (I Sam. 8:4-5)

_____

11. In desiring a king, what did the Lord say they were actually doing? (I Sam. 8:6-8)

_____

12. Was it God's will for Israel to have a king? (I Sam. 12:12-18)

_____

13. Briefly summarize the warning that the Lord gave them concerning the actions of the king who would reign over them. (I Sam. 8:9-17)

_____

14. What did the Lord say that Israel would do because of their oppression, and what would be His response? (I Sam. 8:18)

_____

15. After hearing all this, what did Israel *choose* to do? (I Sam. 8:19-20)

_____

16. As a result of Israel's choice, what did God choose to do? (I Sam. 8:21-22)

_____

Israel rejected God's perfect will for them. They defied God's plan and frustrated His purpose. It was *never* God's will for them to have another king besides Himself. Israel missed God's perfect will for themselves as a nation and moved into His permissive will. They could not, however, prevent God's ultimate plan from being achieved. He now has a Kingdom, a holy nation, and *He is the King*. Because of God's loving kindness and mercy, He continues to try to work with Israel to bring forth His ultimate purpose. However, because of their choice, they reaped the fruit of it and brought upon themselves all the sorrow and misery that God had warned them of.

Let us now examine the life of Saul, their King, to see an example of God's purposes and the free will of the individual.

17. Who chose Saul to be King over Israel? (I Sam. 9:15-17)

_____

18. What choice was set before Saul? (I Sam. 12:24-25)

_____

19. What did Saul choose to do? (I Sam. 13:8-13)

_____

20. What was God's will for Saul? (I Sam. 13:13)

_____

21. Because Saul chose to disobey the Lord, what happened? (I Sam. 13:14)

_____

22. What did the Lord tell Saul to do in the battle with Amalek, and what did Saul choose to do? (I Sam. 15:2-3, 8-9)

_____

23. Because of Saul's choice, what happened? (I Sam. 15:22-28)

_____

Saul's calling and office were ordained by God alone. What God did not ordain was how he would respond to the task He had alloted him.

24. What was God's reaction to Saul's disobedience? (I Sam. 15:11, 35)

_____

25. What is the reason for God's testing of man? (Deut. 8:2)

_____

This is why there are periods of heavy testing before God gives a man responsibility. Through the way men react through trials, God determines faithfulness. It is required of a steward that he be found faithful.

26. When Saul fell away from the office to which God had appointed him, what did God do? (I Sam. 15:28)

_____

27. Before God brought the judgment of Babylonian captivity upon Judah, the Lord had Jeremiah warn them of the coming judgment. What was God's desire? (Jer. 36:2-3)

_____

28. What was the choice of the King and his servants? (Jer. 36:24)

_____

29. The Chaldeans began to besiege Jerusalem. Again, because of His long-suffering and loving kindness, God did not desire that any should perish. God gave them an opportunity to repent. What was God's desire for them? (Jer. 38:2)

_____

The people refused, and the Word of the Lord came to pass.

30. After the deportation to Babylon, there was still a small remnant of Judah in the land. What was the Word of the Lord to them? (Jer. 42:10-19)

_____

31. What was their choice? (Jer. 43:4; Jer. 44:16)

_____

32. In giving Israel all these opportunities to repent, what principle of this loving kindness was the Lord operating under? (Jer. 18:7-10)

_____

33. Does God desire to change His mind about judging people? (Jer. 26:13; Ezk. 24:13)

_____

It is man's free choice to defy God's Word or to repent and obey it. It is God's hope that they will turn to Him and be faithful and enjoy the privileges of His Kingdom.

34. What was God's perfect will and desire for Israel? (Isa. 48:17-19)

_____

   From this study, we have discovered that because of the free choice that God gives every man, the Pharisees, Judas, Saul and Israel as a nation missed God's perfect will for their lives. All four openly defied His Word and rebelled against His counsel. Because they rejected the Word of the Lord to them personally, they fell from their office and their calling and missed their part in God's ultimate purposes for the universe.

35. What exhortation does Peter give? (II Peter 1:10)

_____

36. What eight things are we exhorted to practice that will assure us of never stumbling? (II Peter 1:5-9)

   a _____   e _____
   b _____   f _____
   c _____   g _____
   d _____   h _____

MEMORY VERSE: Deut. 30:19-20

_____
_____
_____
_____
_____

—NOTES—

ANSWERS

"Who is like the wise man and who knows the interpretation of a matter? A man's wisdom illumines him and causes his stern face to beam."

(Ecclesiastes 8:1)

THE ATONEMENT
GOD'S PROVISION FOR MAN'S SIN

Correct Answers

1. They chose to disobey God and rebel against Him.
2. They desired to exalt themselves above God and be God themselves.
3. a. The lust of the flesh (the tree was good for food).
   b. The lust of the eyes (it was a delight to the eyes).
   c. The pride of life (it was desirable to make one wise).
4. He was walking in the garden, calling Adam, and desiring their fellowship.
5. a. None of them are righteous.
   b. None of them understand.
   c. None of them seek for God.
   d. All of them have turned aside and become useless.
   e. None of them does good.
   f. Their mouth is full of death, deceit, poisons, cursing and bitterness.
   g. Their feet are swift to shed blood.
   h. Destruction and misery are in their path.
   i. They have no peace.
   j. They do not fear God.
   k. All of them have sinned and come short of God's glory.
6. God sent a savior and a deliverer, the Son of Man, who came to seek the lost. It is the Spirit of God that draws men unto Him.
7. God's kindness.
8. No.
9. No.
10. As the righteousness which is in the law, he was blameless; yet he was the chief of sinners.
11. Through the law comes the knowledge of sin, that all the world may be accountable to God.
12. By the shedding of the blood of animals.
13. Because in order to make atonement, a sinless sacrifice must be offered.
14. Behold the Lamb of God which takes away the sin of the world.
15. Yes.
16. a. Bore our sins.
    b. Bore our sickness.
    c. Redeemed us from the curse.
    d. Took upon Himself the body of sin, that we may no longer be slaves to it.
17. a. I will put My laws in their minds and write it upon their hearts.
    b. I will be their God and they shall be My people.
    c. They shall know the Lord.
    d. I will be merciful to their iniquities and forget their sins.
    e. Give you a new heart and a new spirit.
    f. He will remove the heart of stone.
18. a. Repent.
    b. Confess Jesus as Lord and believe God raised Him from the dead.
19. To save the world and give them eternal life.
20. Those who have rejected Jesus and who love darkness rather than light.
21. They will be cast into the lake of fire.
22. That none should perish, but all come to repentance and the knowledge of the truth.

REPENTANCE
THE LORDSHIP OF JESUS
THE MESSIAH

Correct Answers

1. That God has made Him both Lord and Christ Messiah.
2. They were pierced to the heart and asked "What shall we do?"
3. a. Repent.
   b. Be baptized.
   c. Receive the gift of the Holy Spirit.
4. Repentance means to confess our sin, turn away from it, forsake it and walk in a new direction; ceasing to do evil and learning to do good.
5. If we confess our sins, He will forgive us and cleanse us from all unrighteousness. We shall be as white as snow and eat the good of the land.
6. We must be willing to make restitution for our wrong-doing, repaying those we owe.
7. He received Jesus gladly, saying that he would give half his possessions to the poor and if he had defrauded anyone, he would give back four times as much.
8. a. This day salvation has come to your house.
   b. The Son of Man came to seek and save that which is lost.
9. a. Do not have fellowship with the ungodly.
   b. Come out from the world and be separate.
   c. Touch not the unclean thing.
10. He squandered his estate with loose living and wound up feeding swine and eating swine food.
11. To leave his sinful ways and the worldly environment and influences to go to his father and confess his sin.
12. He saw him coming and ran to meet him, embraced him and kissed him.
13. He made him a son.
14. a. You shall make no covenant with them.
    b. Show them no favors.
    c. Do not allow your sons and daughters to intermarry with them.
15. a. They will turn your heart away from the Lord.
    b. You are to be a holy people set aside for the Lord alone.
    c. In order that you may live and multiply and go in and possess the land.
16. A marriage relationship.
17. Your God delights and rejoices over you as a bridegroom does his bride.
18. A harlot.
19. a. Adulteresses.
    b. Hostility toward God.
    c. Make yourself an enemy of God.
20. He jealously desires the Spirit He has put in them.
21. The love of the Father is not in them.
22. a. Lust of the flesh.
    b. Lust of the eyes.
    c. The boastful pride of life.
23. They abide forever.
24. a. Love the Lord thy God with all your heart, soul, mind and strength; and love your neighbor as yourself.
    b. Seek the Kingdom of God first, and His righteousness.
25. You must be willing to forsake all.
26. Sit down and count the cost.

27. Eternal life.
28. I have done this, yet what am I lacking?
29. Sell everything, give it away and follow Me.
30. He went away and did not follow Jesus.
31. A sword.
32. a. The religious leaders.
    b. Government officials.
    c. Members of your household.
33. a. Confess with your mouth Jesus as Lord.
    b. Believe in your heart God raised Him from the dead.
34. a. They shall rule and reign with Him.
    b. They shall receive 100 times as much in this present age as they have given up.
    c. They shall receive eternal life in the world to come.
35. He gave them power to become the sons of God.
36. He will come in and have fellowship with us.
37. We are born again.
38. Eternal life.

BAPTISM IN WATER

Correct Answers

1. a. Repent.
   b. Be baptized.
   c. Receive the Holy Spirit.
2. Make disciples of all nations and baptize them.
3. a. That our body of sin might be done away with.
   b. That we should no longer be slaves to sin.
4. By the circumcision of Christ.
5. Burial with Christ in baptism.
6. A sign of the covenant between God and Abraham and his descendants.
7. a. He was cut off from his people.
   b. He has broken God's covenant.
8. Isaac and his descendants.
9. Descendants of Isaac.
10. Those who worship in the Spirit and put no confidence in the flesh.
11. The circumcision of the heart.
12. They were all circumcised.
13. They had not been circumcised in the wilderness.
14. He had rolled away the reproach of Egypt from them.
15. Removal of the body of flesh by the circumcision of Christ.
16. They were baptized in the Sea.
17. a. Burial.
    b. Resurrection.
18. In the likeness of His resurrection.
19. a. To render the devil powerless.
    b. To deliver those who were subject to slavery.
20. They were baptized.
21. They were baptized.
22. He desired baptism.
23. He went down into the water (immersion).
24. He was baptized.
25. Immediately.
26. The same day.
27. In the name of the Father, Son and Holy Spirit.
28. In the name of the Lord Jesus Christ.
29. We are baptized into Jesus Christ.
30. The baptism of repentance.
31. He told him to wash seven times in the Jordan.
32. He was furious and insulted.
33. If the prophet had told you to do some great thing, you would have done it. How much more should you do this simple thing. So Naaman washed and was cleansed.

BAPTISM IN THE HOLY SPIRIT

Correct Answers

1. a. Repent.
   b. Be baptized.
   c. Receive the Holy Spirit.
2. To wait in Jerusalem until they received the promise of the Father and were clothed with power from on High.
3. The baptism of the Holy Spirit.
4. They would receive power to be His witnesses.
5. Jesus fulfilled His ministry under the anointing of the Holy Spirit.
6. He presented Himself alive and by many convincing proofs appeared to them over a period of 40 days, speaking to them of things concerning the Kingdom of God.
7. He abides with you and shall be in you.
8. a. Helper or comforter.
   b. The Spirit of truth.
9. a. He will teach you all things.
   b. He will bring to your remembrance all the things that Jesus said.
   c. He will bear witness of Jesus.
   d. He will guide you into all truth.
   e. He will disclose to you what is to come.
10. His Gospel was not in persuasive words, but in the demonstration of the Spirit and of power.
11. It should not rest on the wisdom of men.
12. The power of God.
13. By the revelation of the Spirit.
14. He will give you what you shall speak.
15. Do not be anxious.
16. a. The Spirit of your Father.
    b. The Spirit of His Son.
17. The women, Mary the mother of Jesus, His brothers.
18. 120.
19. In the temple.
20. Jews from every nation under heaven.
21. a. There came from heaven a noise like a violent rushing wind that filled all the house.
    b. Tongues of fire appeared on them.
    c. They began to speak with tongues as the Spirit gave them utterance.
22. The multitude of Jews there gathered around them, each hearing them speak in their own language.
23. He explained it as the out-pouring of the Holy Spirit spoken of by the prophet Joel.
24. The baptism of fire.
25. He describes it as separating the wheat from the chaff, tossing it up continually until all impurities have been separated from the wheat.
26. The Lord will be like fullers' soap and a refiner's fire. He will purge and purify believers that they may offer unto the Lord offerings of righteousness.
27. To transform us into the same image of the Lord from glory to glory.
28. The Holy Spirit fell on them as they heard Peter's preaching.
29. They heard them speak with tongues and exalt God.
30. Through the laying on of hands.
31. Through the laying on of hands.
32. They spoke in tongues and prophesied.
33. I will put My Spirit within you and cause you to walk in My ordinances.
34. Unto you and your children and to all who are afar off, even as many as the Lord our God shall call.
35. To all His children who ask for it.

Correct Answers

1. A gift.
2. It is given as a pledge of our inheritance with a view to the redemption of God's own possession.
3. To know the one true God.
4. Spirit of adoption as sons entering into a Father-Son relationship.
5. That we are children of God.
6. Those who are being led by the Spirit of God.
7. a. The lame were healed.
   b. Unclean spirits were cast out.
   c. People with palsies and the lame were healed.
   d. Dead were raised.
8. By the power of the Spirit.
9. By the Spirit of God.
10. a. They shall cast out demons.
    b. They shall speak with new tongues.
    c. They shall pick up serpents.
    d. If they drink any deadly poison, it won't hurt them.
    e. They shall lay hands on the sick and they shall recover.
11. The preaching of the Word.
12. Speaking with tongues.
13. Prophecy.
14. a. Speaks to God.
    b. Speaks mysteries.
    c. Edifies himself.
15. The Spirit.
16. No.
17. a. The Spirit intercedes for us according to God's will.
    b. We build ourselves up.
18. He desired for all to speak in tongues and he spoke in tongues more than anyone else.
19. Prophecy.
20. a. He is convicted.
    b. Called to account.
    c. The secrets of his heart are disclosed.
    d. He will fall on his face and worship God.
    e. He will declare that God is among you.
21. The testimony of Jesus.
22. a. Revelation.
    b. Knowledge.
    c. Teaching.
23. Tongues with an interpretation.
24. a. Psalm.
    b. Teaching.
    c. Revelation.
    d. Tongue and interpretation.
25. Sing in the Spirit.
26. a. Varieties of gifts.
    b. Varieties of ministries.
    c. Varieties of effects.

27. a. Word of wisdom.
    b. Word of knowledge.
    c. Faith.
    d. Healing.
    e. Effecting of miracles.
    f. Prophecy.
    g. Distinguishing or discerning of spirits.
    h. Tongues.
    i. Interpretation of tongues.
28. a. Faith, healing and miracles.
    b. Word of knowledge, distinguishing of spirits, word of wisdom.
    c. Faith, healing, miracles.
    d. Discerning of spirits, faith, miracles.
    e. Word of knowledge, prophecy.
    f. Tongues and interpretation of tongues.
29. Word of wisdom.
30. a. Apostles.
    b. Prophets.
    c. Evangelists.
    d. Pastors.
    e. Teachers.
    f. Workers of miracles.
    g. Gifts of healings.
    h. Helps.
    i. Administrations.
    j. Various kinds of tongues.
31. a. Service.
    b. Exhortation—encouragement.
    c. Giving.
    d. Leading—giving aid.
    e. Showing mercy.
    f. Contributing to the needs of the saints.
    g. Practicing hospitality.
32. a. Love.
    b. Joy.
    c. Peace.
    d. Patience.
    e. Kindness.
    f. Goodness.
    g. Faithfulness.
    h. Gentleness.
    i. Self-control.
33. No.
34. No.
35. a. Prophecy.
    b. Visions.
    c. Dreams.
36. For the common good.
37. From your innermost being shall flow rivers of living water which shall be a well of water springing up to eternal life.

THE AUTHORITY OF GOD'S WORD

Correct Answers

1. a. Inspired by God.
   b. Men moved by the Holy Spirit spoke from God.
2. a. Teaching.
   b. Reproof.
   c. Correction.
   d. Training in righteousness.
3. a. Desire the sincere milk of the Word.
   b. Study to show yourselves approved unto God a master workman, dividing the Word accurately.
4. We will grow in respect to salvation.
5. The Word of God.
6. Why do you call me Lord, Lord, and do not do the things that I say?
7. We must destroy speculations and everything raised above the knowledge of God, bringing every thought captive to the obedience of Christ.
8. Every word that proceeds from the mouth of God.
9. Blinded the minds of the unbelieving.
10. By the renewing of your mind by the washing of the water of the Word.
11. a. A glorious church without spot or wrinkle.
    b. Holy and blameless.
    c. In the same image of Jesus.
12. Ignorance of the Word.
13. For the lack of knowledge.
14. God will reject us from being His priests and forget our children.
15. A lamp to my feet and a light to my path.
16. a. Makes us wiser than our enemies.
    b. Gives us more insight than our teachers.
    c. Gives us more understanding than the aged.
17. By keeping God's Word and treasuring it in your heart.
18. a. Liberty.
    b. Boldness.
19. God's Word is sweeter to him than honey.
20. The joy and rejoicing of his heart.
21. More than his necessary food.
22. a. Forever Thy Word is settled in heaven.
    b. The sum of Thy Word is truth.
    c. God will not lie, but will do what He has spoken.
    d. Heaven and earth will pass away, but My Word will not pass away.
23. a. Give attention to God's Word.
    b. Incline your ear to His sayings.
    c. Do not let them depart from your sight.
    d. Keep them in the midst of your heart.
24. a. He will be like a tree firmly planted by streams of water.
    b. He will yield fruit in season.
    c. His leaf will not wither.
    d. Whatever he does shall prosper.
25. a. The Word shall be in your mouth.
    b. Meditate on it day and night.
    c. Be careful to do it.

26. a. Impress these words in your heart and soul.
    b. Bind them as a sign on your hand.
    c. They shall be as frontals on your forehead.
    d. Teach them to your sons.
    e. Talk of them when you sit in your house, when you are walking, lying down and when you rise up.
    f. Write them on the doorposts of your house and on your gates.
27. a. That your sons may fill the land and remain in it forever.
    b. The Lord will drive out all your enemies before you.
    c. Every place on which the sole of your foot treads shall be yours.
    d. No man shall be able to stand before you. The fear and dread of you shall fall on all people.
28. The sword of the Spirit.
29. a. It is living, active and sharper than any two-edged sword.
    b. It divides the soul and spirit, joints and marrow.
    c. It is able to judge the thoughts and intentions of the heart.
    d. All things are revealed before it and nothing can hide from it.
30. By the Word of God.
31. By keeping His Word.
32. The wise man hears the Word of God and does it. Through the storm and flood, his house stands because it is founded on the rock.
33. The foolish man hears the Word of God and does not do it. His house falls when the storm comes because it was built on sand.
34. Those who hear the Word of God and do it.
35. a. Builds you up.
    b. Gives you an inheritance among the saints.
    c. Through it you partake of the divine nature.
    d. Through it you escape the corruption that is in the world by lust.

PRAISE, WORSHIP AND PRAYER

Correct Answers

1. He is worthy to be praised.
2. To declare His praise.
3. Continually.
4. Everything that has breath.
5. He who offers a sacrifice of thanksgiving.
6. a. Clap your hands.
   b. Shout joyfully.
   c. Sing praises.
7. a. Trumpet.
   b. Harp.
   c. Lyre.
   d. Timbrel.
   e. Stringed instruments.
   f. Pipe.
   g. Loud and resounding cymbals.
8. a. With a new song.
   b. With dancing.
9. The high praises of God.
10. To bind the satanic hosts.
11. The enemy was routed and they began to destroy one another.
12. The Lord is enthroned upon our praises.
13. The fallen tabernacle of David.
14. Among men.
15. Praise and worship.
16. Those who worship Him in spirit and truth.
17. In reverence.
18. Bowing before Him.
19. a. They sang praises with joy.
    b. They bowed down and worshiped.
20. Holy array—the beauty of holiness.
21. a. Ask in My name.
    b. You shall receive.
    c. So that your joy may be full.
22. Not to use meaningless repetitions.
23. Because they suppose that they will be heard for their many words.
24. He knows your need before you even ask.
25. We must forgive those whom we have something against.
26. You should believe that you have received them.
27. They shall be granted unto you.
28. a. Because you do not ask.
    b. Because you ask with wrong motives.
29. a. One who is God-fearing.
    b. One who does God's will.
30. To pray and not lose heart.
31. He gave her the request because she kept bothering him.

32. He will not delay over the prayers of His elect, but will bring about justice for them speedily.
33. Faith.
34. a. Ask and you shall receive.
    b. Seek and you shall find.
    c. Knock and it shall be opened unto you.
35. He will give what is good to those who ask Him.
36. The prayer of the upright.
37. The sacrifice of the wicked.
38. Ask what you will and it shall be done.
39. a. Regarding iniquity in your heart.
    b. Wavering—doubting.
    c. Not giving honor to your wife.
40. Let your requests be made known to God.
41. In prayer.
42. The blood of Jesus.
43. Intercedes for us according to God's will.
44. Fasting.
45. It shall be done for them.
46. Pray for kings and all who are in authority.
47. a. In order that we may lead a tranquil and quiet life in all godliness and dignity.
    b. In order that all men may have an opportunity to be saved and come to the knowledge of the truth.
48. a. Lift up holy hands.
    b. Avoid wrath and dissension.
49. Always, without ceasing.

GOD'S PROVISION FOR HEALING

Correct Answers

1. Because man sinned.
2. The devil.
3. He would allow none of the diseases of the Egyptians (the world) to come upon them.
4. By His scourgings, or stripes, we are healed.
5. By His wounds, we were healed.
6. To destroy the works of the devil.
7. a. Bless their bread and water.
   b. Take sickness away from them.
8. a. Forgave him of all his iniquities.
   b. Healed all his diseases.
9. All of them.
10. For all those who hate God's people.
11. For those who do not obey God's Word and those who do not fear His name.
12. a. Extraordinary plagues (severe and lasting).
    b. Miserable and chronic sicknesses.
    c. All the diseases in Egypt.
    d. Every sickness and every plague.
13. That we might choose the blessing and choose life.
14. a. Love the Lord.
    b. Obey His voice.
    c. Hold fast to Him.
15. a. No evil will befall you.
    b. No plague will come near your dwelling.
16. a. Health and healing.
    b. He will reveal to them an abundance of peace and truth.
17. To do good and heal all who were oppressed by the devil.
18. All of them.
19. All kinds.
20. The unbelief of the people.
21. a. They recognized the Lordship of Jesus.
    b. They had faith in His Word.
22. His Word.
23. Only say the word and my servant shall be healed.
24. a. He had never seen greater faith.
    b. He received what he had believed for.
25. Faith.
26. Through faith in Jesus' name, this man had been healed.
27. a. Heal the sick.
    b. Raise the dead.
    c. Cleanse the leper.
    d. Cast out demons.
28. a. The things that He did.
    b. Even greater works.
29. a. In the name of Jesus.
    b. Laying on of hands.
30. Yes.

31. a. Pray over him.
    b. Anoint with oil in the name of Jesus.
32. a. Heal him.
    b. If he has committed any sins, they will be forgiven.
33. The prayer of faith.
34. Sin.
35. His body wasted away and his vitality was drained.
36. He walked before the Lord in truth with his whole heart and did what was right in God's sight.
37. The Lord heard his prayer and added 15 years to his life.
38. He followed the Lord, but not fully, for he put his trust in the arm of the flesh—in men and not in God. He also imprisoned the seer of the Lord.
39. He became seriously diseased in the feet.
40. He failed to seek the Lord and he died.
41. They have not asked.
42. They asked.
43. Ask in faith and you shall receive, that your joy may be full.
44. Healing.

GOD'S PLAN FOR INNER HEALING AND DELIVERANCE

Correct Answers

1. Mentally confused, sick at heart, full of raw wounds, bruised, with welts not healed, full of sin, in bad health, festering wounds, mourning, benumbed, badly crushed, agitated in the heart, full of anxiety.
2. He desires to restore our soul.
3. By the renewing of your mind.
4. By the anointing of the Spirit.
5. a. Comfort My people, declaring that her warfare is ended and her iniquity has been removed.
   b. Clear the way for the Lord.
   c. Make smooth in the desert a highway for our God.
   d. Let every valley be lifted up and every mountain be made low.
   e. Let the rough ground become a plain and the rugged terrain a broad valley.
   f. Then the glory of the Lord will be revealed and all flesh shall see it together.
6. Build up, prepare the way, remove every obstacle out of the way of My people.
7. a. A glorious church without spot or wrinkle.
   b. By the washing of the water of the Word.
8. The insides were washed with water.
9. Truth.
10. The shepherds.
11. The favorable year of the Lord.
12. a. Awake and clothe yourself in strength and beautiful garments.
    b. Shake yourself from the dust, O captive.
    c. Loose yourself from the chains around your neck.

I. Inner Healing

1. He desires for them to be pressed out, bandaged and softened with oil or ointment.
2. It is like purified oil or ointment poured forth.
3. By the revelation of the Lord.
4. He will reveal it.
5. The word of knowledge.
6. Confess your sins one to another and pray for one another that you may be healed.
7. Must be willing to forgive that person who has hurt him.
8. He bore our griefs and carried our sorrows.
9. a. To bind up the broken-hearted.
   b. To comfort all who mourn.
   c. To set at liberty those who are bruised.
10. a. A garland.
    b. The oil of gladness.
11. The mantle of praise.
12. I will heal him, restore comfort and peace to him and create praise in his lips.

II. Deliverance

1. He rendered powerless the devil that we might be delivered from bondage.
2. Cast them out.
3. The name of Jesus.
4. His iniquities will capture him and he will be held by the cords of his sin.
5. Lack of instruction.

6. Woe to those who drag iniquity and sin around with them.
7. Falsehood.
8. Because of the lusts of deceit.
9. They shall not prosper.
10. Confess and forsake them.
11. Those who had believed kept coming, confessing and disclosing their practices.
12. a. Take away all the strong man's armor on which he has relied.
    b. Distribute his plunder.
13. The coming of the Kingdom of God.
14. a. Being overcome by a certain sin or habit.
    b. Unforgiveness.
    c. The iniquities of the fathers.
15. The Lord hands them over to the torturers.
16. You must forgive from your heart.
17. He will not forgive you.
18. a. You lay aside the old manner of life which is corrupted by the lust of deceit.
    b. You become renewed in the spirit of your mind.
    c. You put on the new self which is in the likeness of God.
19. a. In the likeness of God.
    b. Created in righteousness.
    c. Created in holiness of the truth.
20. a. Bitter jealousy.
    b. Selfish ambition.
21. The root of bitterness.
22. a. Knowledge of the Word of God.
    b. Supernatural revelation of the Lord.
23. a. Word of knowledge.
    b. Discerning of spirits.
24. a. To proclaim liberty to the captives.
    b. To proclaim freedom to the prisoners.

III. Breaking of Curses.
 1. He became a curse for us.
 2. That the blessing of Abraham might come upon the Gentiles through faith.
 3. a. Blessed are those whose lawless deeds have been forgiven.
    b. Blessed are those whose sins have been covered.
    c. Blessed is the man whose sin the Lord will not take into account.
 4. a. Life and prosperity—the blessing.
    b. Death and adversity—the curse.
 5. If they went and served other gods.
 6. The third and fourth generations of those who hated God.
 7. Blessings and loving kindness to thousands.
 8. a. Idolatry—witchcraft.
    b. Dishonoring father and mother.
    c. Moving your neighbor's boundary mark (cheating your neighbor).
    d. Misleading a blind person (being cruel to the disabled).
    e. Those who distort justice due to an alien, orphan, or widow (taking advantage of the helpless).
    f. Lying with your father's wife.
    g. Lying with an animal.
    h. Incest.
    i. Lying with your mother-in-law.
    j. Striking your neighbor in secret.
    k. Accepting a bribe.
    l. Refusing to obey the Lord or to keep His commandments.

9. They will be a sign and a wonder upon your descendants forever.
10. Through ignorance.
11. a. Cursed in the city and in the country.
    b. Your food supply shall be cursed.
    c. Your children, your animals and the produce of your ground shall be cursed.
    d. You shall be cursed when you come in and when you go out.
    e. Confusion.
    f. Rebuke.
    g. You shall not prosper.
    h. Oppressed and robbed continually.
    i. Others shall eat up your labors.
    j. You shall be oppressed and crushed continually.
12. a. Boils.
    b. Hemorrhoids.
    c. Scab.
    d. Itch.
    e. Sore boils on knees and legs.
    f. Boils from head to foot.
    g. Severe, lasting, extraordinary plagues.
    h. Miserable and chronic sicknesses.
13. a. Madness.
    b. Bewilderment of heart.
    c. Feelings of being driven mad.
    d. Despair of soul (sorrow of mind).
    e. Doubt, dread and fear.
14. The curse of bad and oppressive governments.
15. The curse of adultery and divorce.
16. The curse of illegitimate birth going down ten generations which shall be rejected by the assembly of the Lord.
17. You will serve your enemies in hunger, thirst, nakedness and the lack of all things and He will put an iron yoke on your neck until He has destroyed you.
18. a. Rebuilding the ancient ruins.
    b. Raising up the former devastations.
    c. Repairing the desolations of many generations.
19. As one who has lifted the yoke from us and fed us.
20. Their descendants will be recognized as the offspring which the Lord has blessed.
21. My soul will exult in God, for He has clothed me with the garments of salvation and wrapped me with a robe of righteousness.

PRINCIPLES THAT BUILD CHARACTER

Correct Answers

1. Adultery.
2. No, let your statement be yes or no.
3. Evil.
4. We will be held accountable on the day of judgment.
5. By our words.
6. What is in the heart.
7. Do not resist him but turn the other cheek.
8. He did not revile or threaten but committed Himself to God.
9. You are to rejoice and be exceedingly glad.
10. Love your enemies and pray for them.
11. He sends sun and rain on the evil men and on the good men.
12. Be merciful as the Father is merciful.
13. No.
14. No.
15. *The Offense*   *The Guilt*
    a. angry with your brother   guilty before the court
    b. calling your brother "Raca"   guilty before the Supreme Court
    c. calling your brother a fool   guilty enough to go into hell fire
16. You will be judged.
17. By the same standard with which you judge others.
18. a. Do not pass judgment and you will not be judged.
    b. Do not condemn and you will not be condemned.
    c. Pardon and you will be pardoned.
19. Go and first be reconciled to your brother, then come and offer your gift.
20. Beware of practicing your righteousness before men to be noticed by them.
21. You should give secretly.
22. He will not forgive you.
23. 70 times 7.
24. As we would have them treat us.
25. a. Whoever takes your coat, give him your shirt also.
    b. Whoever takes away what is yours, do not demand it back.
    c. Lend expecting nothing in return.
26. Be on guard against every form of greed.
27. He who is faithful in a very little is also faithful in much.
28. He who is unfaithful in a very little is also unfaithful in much.
29. The humble attitude.
30. He will be humbled.
31. Become a servant.
32. He did not come to be served but to serve and give His life for many.
33. No, take the last place for yourself.
34. The poor, the crippled, the lame, the blind, and those who do not have the means to repay.
35. To lay down your life for your friends.
36. Shepherd My sheep and tend My lambs.
37. a. Feed the hungry.
    b. Give water to the thirsty.
    c. Invite in the stranger.
    d. Clothe the naked.
    e. Visit the sick.
    f. Visit those in prison.

38. Let us not love in word but in deed and truth.
39. a. The poor in spirit.
    b. Those who mourn (repentant).
    c. The gentle.
    d. Those who hunger and thirst after righteousness.
    e. The merciful.
    f. The pure in heart.
    g. The peacemakers.
    h. Those who are persecuted for righteousness' sake.
    i. Those who men revile, persecute and say all manner of evil against falsely on account of Jesus.

GOD'S PERFECT CHOICE

Correct Answers

1. Marriage.
2. God.
3. God.
4. Beautiful and a virgin.
5. She was willing to go.
6. Meditating.
7. No.
8. He loved God's choice.
9. a. Lust of the flesh.
   b. Lust of the eyes.
   c. Boastful pride of life.
10. The one who does the will of God abides forever.
11. a. Flee from youthful lusts.
    b. Appeal to younger men as brothers, younger women as sisters in all purity.
    c. Flee immorality.
    d. Conduct yourself in holiness, not lustful passion.
12. The things of the Lord, how you may please the Lord. Seek first the Kingdom.
13. Do not be conformed to this world. Live sensibly, righteously, and godly in this present age.
14. God will give good to those who ask Him.
15. a. Delight yourself in the Lord, commit your way to the Lord, rest in the Lord, wait patiently for Him.
    b. He who finds a wife finds a good thing and obtains favor from the Lord.
    c. No good thing will He withhold from those who walk uprightly.
    d. A prudent wife is from the Lord.
16. The will of God.

COMMITMENT TO THE BODY
OF THE MESSIAH JESUS

Correct Answers

1. If we have love for one another.
2. To love one another as He has loved us.
3. Laying down your life for our brothers.
4. a. Loyalty and fervent devotion to each other.
   b. Restraint from backbiting and devouring one another.
   c. Esteeming your brother better than yourself.
   d. The strong are to bear the burdens of the weak. When one member suffers, all suffer with it. When one member is honored, all members rejoice with it.
   e. Loving your enemies.
   f. Opening your life and sharing your life—your victories and defeats before all with all.
   g. Loving in deed and if any has need, your abundance is available to supply their wants.
5. The unity of the Spirit in the bond of peace.
6. A house divided against itself fails and a kingdom divided against itself is laid waste.
7. Go and be reconciled to your brother, then come and present your offering.
8. Receive, forgive and love everyone as Christ has received, forgiven and loved you.
9. One body.
10. The body is not one member, but many.
11. No.
12. In the body, just as He desired.
13. No.
14. For the common good.
15. By that which every joint supplies.
16. Proper working order.
17. The body will grow and build itself up in love.
18. The Lord's army has unity, order and discipline which allows them to do great things for God.
19. We are living stones and we are growing into a holy temple in the Lord and are being built together into a dwelling of God in the Spirit and a spiritual house for a holy priesthood.
20. He is building His church and the gates of hell shall not overpower it.
21. A glorious church.
22. In the church.
23. Through the church.
24. The vine.
25. The branches.
26. Abide in Jesus and in relationship with His body.
27. They received the Word, were baptized, continually devoted themselves to the apostles's teaching, to fellowship, to the breaking of bread and prayer. Many signs and wonders took place as they continually felt a sense of awe. They had all things in common, distributing to those who had need. They were with one mind, with gladness and sincerity of heart praising God. The Lord was adding to their number day by day.

Correct Answers

1. a. Apostles.
   b. Prophets.
   c. Evangelists.
   d. Pastors.
   e. Teachers.
2. a. To equip the saints for the work of service.
   b. To build up the body of Christ.
3. Until we attain unto the unity of the faith, the knowledge of the Son of God, to a mature man and the measure of the stature of the fullness of Christ.
4. We will no longer be children who are tossed and deceived, but will speak the truth and grow up into Him.
5. Elders.
6. a. Be on guard for the flock.
   b. Shepherd them.
   c. Watch over their souls.
   d. Give an account.
7. To see the sword coming and warn the people.
8. The watchmen are held accountable.
9. Those who refuse to listen.
10. a. Obey them.
    b. Submit to them.
11. God.
12. a. We are resisting the ordinance of God.
    b. Will receive condemnation upon themselves.
13. a. Rebellion is as the sin of divination.
    b. Insubordination is as iniquity and idolatry.
14. Observe their way of life and imitate their faith.
15. Do what is good and right.
16. We should fear, for He will bring wrath upon those who practice evil.
17. a. If a brother sins, go and reprove him.
    b. If he refuses to listen, take one or two more with you.
    c. If he refuses to listen to them, take it to the church.
    d. If he refuses to listen to the church, let him be as a Gentile and sinner.
18. Evil and sin like leaven filters through the whole lump.
19. Clean out the old leaven of malice and wickedness.
20. Any so-called brother who is immoral, covetous, idolater, reviler, drunkard, swindler.
21. a. We are to judge those who are within the church.
    b. God judges those who are without the church; the sinners.
22. Remove the wicked man from among yourselves.
23. It's better to get rid of even the most important members of the body than to cause the whole body to go into Hell because of the spreading wickedness.
24. They fled, 36 men were killed.

25. They took some things under the ban, both having deceived and stolen.
26. The things from under the ban and the people who took them were to be burned with fire.
27. That God loves us and that we are His sons.
28. a. For our good.
    b. That we may share His holiness.
29. For the moment it seems not to be joyful, but sorrowful.
30. It yields the peaceful fruit of righteousness.
31. He divided them into 1,000, 100, 50, and 10 and put leaders over each of them.
32. He alone was counseling the people from morning till evening and the people had to wait for long hours. He and the people were wearing themselves out.
33. a. They must know the statutes, laws and ways of God.
    b. Able men who fear God.
    c. Men of truth.
    d. Hate dishonest gain.
    e. Wise.
    f. Discerning.
    g. Experienced.
34. To settle every minor dispute and help bear Moses' burden.
35. Every difficult and major dispute.
36. a. With no partiality, for the judgment is God's.
    b. Not by what the eyes see or what the ears hear.
    c. With righteousness and fairness.
37. The older women. (Note: this is not necessarily older with age, but older in spiritual maturity.)

PROSPERITY AND GIVING

Correct Answers

1. a. Pay God His tithes and contributions.
   b. Seek the Kingdom of God first and His righteousness.
2. In tithes and offerings or contributions.
3. The tenth.
4. a. The land.
   b. The seed of the land.
   c. The fruit of the tree.
   d. The herd and the flock.
5. It is determined according to the willingness and leading of the heart.
6. We come under a curse.
7. In the storehouse where it is to be given to the priests and Levites.
8. Food for God's house and to provide for the needs of the ministry and those who perform the service of the Lord.
9. Yes.
10. He will open the windows of heaven and pour out a blessing until there is no more need.
11. The devourer.
12. He was blessed in every way.
13. Your barns will be filled with plenty and your vats will overflow with wine.
14. a. Protection.
    b. Food.
    c. Clothing.
15. Give tenth of all.
16. God dealt graciously with him and he had plenty.
17. Give and it will be given to you in good measure, pressed down, shaken together, and running over.
18. In the same measure that you give.
19. He who sows sparingly, reaps sparingly.
20. Do not give grudgingly or under compulsion.
21. God loves a cheerful giver.
22. a. To give you a sufficiency in everything.
    b. To give you an abundance for every good deed.
23. a. Seed to the sower.
    b. Bread for food.
24. Every form of greed.
25. The abundance of possessions.
26. He was greedy and God required his life.
27. The man who lays up treasure for himself is not rich toward God.
28. Riches being hoarded by the owner for his own hurt.
29. The deceitfulness of riches.
30. a. Those who give out of their surplus.
    b. Those who give sacrificially, giving all that they have to live on.
31. The widow who gave sacrificially.
32. Do not set your heart upon them.
33. Where your treasure is.
34. Lay up treasures in heaven rather than on earth.
35. The love of money.

36. a. Fall into temptation and a snare and many foolish and harmful desires which bring ruin and destruction.
    b. Some have wandered away from the faith.
    c. They have pierced themselves with many a pang.
37. He will be prosperous.
38. a. You will be enriched in everything for all liberality.
    b. Many thanksgivings will be given to God by those whose needs have been met by your giving.
    c. You will be fully supplying the needs of the saints.
39. It is proof of your obedience to your confession of the Gospel of Christ.
40. a. What you shall eat.
    b. What you shall drink.
    c. What you shall wear.
41. The Gentiles or unbelievers.
42. The Kingdom of God and His righteousness.
43. All these things will be added unto you.
44. Wisdom, knowledge and joy.
45. The task of gathering and collecting so that God may give to the one who is good in His sight.
46. The things above.
47. He was a successful man.
48. The Lord was with him.
49. His soul will abide in prosperity.
50. Wisdom and knowledge to rule God's people.
51. God granted him wisdom and knowledge and gave him riches, wealth and honor.
52. Every good thing.
53. Everything they need so that there is no lack.
54. a. He does not walk in the counsel of the wicked.
    b. He does not stand in the path of sinners.
    c. He does not sit in the seat of scoffers.
    d. He delights in and meditates in the Word day and night.
    e. He is like a tree planted by streams of water, producing fruit in its season; his leaf does not wither.

THE GREAT COMMISSION

Correct Answers

1. Follow Me, and I will make you fishers of men.
2. Repentance and the Gospel of the Kingdom of God.
3. a. To preach repentance and the forgiveness of sins to all nations.
   b. Making disciples of all nations.
   c. Baptizing them.
   d. Teaching them to observe all that I have commanded you.
4. Jesus and the resurrection of the dead.
5. To be a witness for Him to all men.
6. He testified to both small and great.
7. Power to be His witnesses.
8. Wins souls.
9. He became all things to all men that he might save some. He did all things for the sake of the Gospel.
10. Once I was blind, but now I see. If He were not from God, He could do nothing.
11. They put him out of the synagogue.
12. a. Religious leaders.
    b. Government officials.
    c. Members of our household.
13. It shall be given you what you shall speak.
14. The Spirit of your Father.
15. They were unable to cope with the wisdom and the spirit with which he was speaking.
16. a. Make known His deeds among the peoples.
    b. Speak of all His wonders.
17. Do not be afraid, but go on speaking and do not be silent.
18. It brings a snare.
19. Stand in the temple and speak to the people the whole message.
20. We must obey God rather than men.
21. Do not be ashamed, but join with me in suffering for the gospel according to the power of God.
22. He will confess us before the Father.
23. He will deny us before the Father.
24. a. What I tell you in darkness, speak in the light.
    b. What you hear whispered in your ear, proclaim upon the housetop.
    c. Do not fear men who would kill you, but fear God.
25. He did not shrink back from declaring to them the whole purpose of God.
26. He did not consider his life as dear to himself in order that he might finish his course and the ministry which God had given him.
27. a. I have fought the good fight.
    b. I have finished the course.
    c. I have kept the faith.
    d. There is laid up for me a crown of righteousness.
28. The crown of righteousness.
29. They will shine as the stars forever and ever.

30. a. Save the sinner's soul from death.
    b. Cover a multitude of sins.
31. a. They shall reap with joyful shouting.
    b. They shall return bringing their sheaves with them.
32. He felt compassion for them for they were distressed and downcast like sheep without a shepherd.
33. The harvest is plentiful but the workers are few.
34. Pray for the Lord of the harvest to send out workers into His harvest.
35. a. Those who sow beside all waters.
    b. Those who send forth disciples or workers freely.
36. Do not put it off, for the fields are ripe *NOW,* ready for harvest.
37. One sows, another reaps, one plants, another waters, but it is God who gives the increase.
38. Each will receive his own reward according to his own labor.
39. As his share is who goes down to the battle, so shall his share be who stays with the baggage.
40. They have entered into the labor of others.
41. Rejoice together.
42. a. By the blood of the Lamb.
    b. By the word of your testimony.
    c. Loving not your life even unto death.
43. We should suffer hardship as a good soldier.
44. We should avoid entangling ourselves with the affairs of everyday life.
45. An athlete and a hard-working farmer.
46. We should endure all things for the sake of those who are chosen that they may obtain salvation.

THE LAST DAYS AND THE RETURN
OF THE MESSIAH JESUS

Correct Answers

1. He will come again in the same manner as you have watched Him go.
2. a. The dead in Christ will rise first.
   b. Those who are alive and remain will be caught up to meet the Lord.
3. The physical body will be changed to an immortal and imperishable body.
4. Death.
5. Until He has put all enemies under His feet.
6. Death.
7. A progressive transformation into the likeness of Jesus.
8. No; the change is from glory to glory.
9. a. A church in all her glory.
   b. Having no spot or wrinkle.
   c. Holy and blameless.
10. By the washing of the water of the Word.
11. To be conformed to the image of the Son.
12. To put on the new self.
13. The bride has made herself ready.
14. The righteous acts of the saints.
15. They purify themselves just as He is pure.
16. a. Deny ungodliness and worldly desires.
    b. Live sensibly, righteously and godly.
17. a. The church going forth into the world as Jesus went forth.
    b. The same unity that Jesus had with the Father. (This unity will be between each member of the body for one another and between each believer and God.)
    c. The same glory that Jesus had.
    d. Perfection into a unity.
18. a. He did nothing of Himself, but only what He saw the Father doing.
    b. The Father showed Him all things.
    c. He judged as He heard from God.
    d. He did not seek His own will, but the will of God.
    e. He did not speak His own words, but only what the Father told Him to speak.
    f. Those who beheld Him, beheld God.
    g. The world found no guilt in Him.
19. a. They were not defiled with women (harlot systems).
    b. They follow the Lamb wherever He goes.
    c. No lie was found in their mouth.
    d. They are blameless.
20. Be dressed in readiness, keeping your lamps alight, waiting and watching.
21. Faithful Servant: Faithful and sensible steward who was feeding the flock and doing the Master's will.
    Reward: He is put in charge of all the master's possessions.
    Drunken Servant: He says that the Master won't come for a long time. He mistreats others and is a glutton and drunkard satisfying his own lusts.
    Reward: The Lord will come on a day which the slave will not know about. He will cut him in pieces.

Lazy Servant: He knew his Master's will, but did not do it or get ready and did not act according to God's will.
Reward: He shall receive many lashes or blows.
Ignorant Servant: He did not know the Master's will and committed deeds worthy of flogging.
Reward: He will receive a few lashes.

22. Those who were prepared, ready and on the alert.
23. As a thief in the night.
24. Not as a thief; for we are not of the darkness, but of the light.
25. He will do nothing unless He reveals His secret counsel to His servants the prophets.

ANOTHER LOOK AT THE LAST DAYS

Correct Answers

1. Like the days of Noah.
2. The cares of this life and with satisfying the lust of the flesh.
3. The wicked.
4. The wicked.
5. The righteous.
6. a. The upright and blameless will remain.
   b. The wicked and treacherous will be cut off and rooted out of the earth.
7. The sinners.
8. The gentle.
9. The things that cannot be shaken.
10. The kingdom which cannot be shaken.
11. a. The sinners and the godless.
    b. The righteous and sincere.
12. Those whose hearts are weighted down with dissatisfaction, drunkeness and the worries of life.
13. Be on the alert and pray that you may have strength to escape these things and to stand before the Son of Man.
14. That they not be taken out of the world, but kept from the evil one.
15. Remember Lot's wife—do not grasp for earthly things.
16. a. False Christ and false prophets.
    b. Great international wars.
    c. Famines and earthquakes.
    d. Christians killed and hated.
    e. Many will fall away and betray one another.
    f. Lawlessness will increase.
    g. People's love will grow cold.
    h. The Gospel of the Kingdom will be preached to all nations.
17. a. The rise of Zionism and the rebuilding of the state of Israel.
    b. Jerusalem liberated from Gentile dominion.
18. Until the period of restoration of all things about which God spoke by the mouth of His holy prophets from ancient time.
19. a. The nations turning to Jesus, His resting place (the church) will be glorious.
    b. Recovering of the dispersed Jews from the four corners of the earth.
21. The Lord who brought up and led back the descendants of Israel from the North land and from all the countries where He had driven them.
22. The New Covenant.
23. The city of Jerusalem shall be rebuilt and it shall never be plucked up or overthrown any more.
24. a. The Righteous Branch (the church) will spring forth.
    b. Judah will be saved.
25. a. The coming in of the Gentiles into the Kingdom.
    b. Israel will return to their land and seek the Lord.
26. In the last days.

27. When the fulness of the Gentiles has come in, all of Israel will be saved and grafted back in.
28. Multitudes will be saved, nations and kings will come into the Kingdom of God.
29. In order that the nations may know the Lord.
30. a. An earthquake.
    b. Every man's sword will be against his brother (they will turn on one another).
    c. A rain of hailstones, fire and brimstone.
31. That the Lord has done it. That He lives.
32. They will acknowledge that the Lord is their God from that day onward.
33. That the house of Israel went into exile because they had turned away from the Lord.
34. They will forget all the animosity they had toward Jesus and will know that it was God that sent them into exile.
35. He will pour out His Spirit upon the house of Israel.
36. The house of Judah first, then the inhabitants of Jerusalem.
37. They will recognize Him whom they have pierced, who is Jesus, and they will mourn for Him as one mourns for his only son.
38. A fountain for sin and for impurity for the house of David.
39. When they say, "Blessed is He Who comes in the name of the Lord".
40. Those who overcome and have forsaken all to follow Him.

FAITH TOWARD GOD

Correct Answers

1. a. Repentance from dead works.
   b. Faith toward God.
   c. Instruction about washings.
   d. Laying on of hands.
   e. The resurrection of the dead.
   f. Eternal judgment.
2. Without faith, it is impossible to please God.
3. The man who comes to God must believe:
   a. That He is (exists).
   b. That He is a rewarder of those who diligently seek Him.
4. It is by grace, through faith.
5. Faith comes by hearing the Word of God.
6. a. Confess.
   b. Believe.
   c. Accept.
7. He was to tell him words by which he and his household would be saved.
8. Paul: a. He preached the Gospel.
          b. He perceived that the man had faith to be healed.
          c. He told the man to stand up and walk.
   The man: a. He heard Paul preach.
          b. He had faith to be healed.
          c. He leaped and walked.
9. He heard the words that Paul spoke.
10. Faith is the assurance of things hoped for, the conviction of things not seen.
11. By faith God made the world by His Word, so that what is seen was not made out of things that are visible.
12. a. Confess or say it.
    b. Do not doubt in your heart.
    c. Believe that what you say is going to happen.
    d. Receive—it shall be granted.
13. a. God believed it.
    b. He said it.
    c. It happened or came to pass—it materialized.
14. You must first believe that you received them and then it shall be given.
15. Thomas had seen the nails pierce Jesus' hands and the spear thrust into His side. His physical senses told him that Jesus was dead. Thomas was using head knowledge rather than faith.
16. Thomas believed when he had seen.
17. Blessed are they that have not seen, and yet have believed.
18. a. He believed God, who calls things into being which do not exist.
    b. Against hope, he believed according to that which God had spoken.
    c. Without becoming weak in faith, he did not consider the circumstances.
    d. He did not waver in unbelief, but grew strong in faith.
    e. He was fully assured that what God had promised; He was able to perform.
19. He considered the Word of God.
20. By receiving God's Word as the word of a friend.
21. Received God's Word as she did the word of her friend.
22. God does not lie, He has spoken it, He will make it good.

FAITH IS LOOKING CONTINUALLY AT THE WORD
AND BEING A DOER OF IT

Correct Answers

1. By inclining your ear to His Word and keeping God's Word before your eyes and in the midst of your heart.
2. He refused the circumstances and looked intently at God's promise.
3. God's Word shall succeed.
4. His confession.
5. If we believe what we say shall come to pass, we can have whatever we say.
6. No, we must say it.
7. a. The blood of the Lamb.
   b. The words of our testimony.
   c. Loving not our life unto death.
8. He had given the city of Jericho into his hand.
9. No.
10. Seven priests carry rams' horns before the ark. Go around the city with the army once a day for six days. On the seventh day, march around seven times with the priests blowing the trumpets. When the priests make a long blast with the rams' horns, the people shall shout and the walls will fall. Then go in and take the city, destroying everything.
11. No.
12. They climbed up on the roof, cut a hole in it and let him down.
13. He saw their faith.
14. He obeyed the Words of the Lord and acted out his faith in that Word.
15. To be a doer of the Word and not a hearer only.
16. By works.
17. By offering up Isaac.
18. He believed that God who had said that through Isaac his seed should come, was able to raise him from the dead.
19. By preparing the ark, acting on what God had told him.
20. By works.
21. One who looks in the mirror and walks away, forgetting what he looks like.
22. a. Look intently at the Word.
    b. Abide by it.
    c. Be an effectual doer of it.
23. We will be blessed in what we do.

THE CONFESSION OF GOD'S WORD BUILDS FAITH
AND FIXES THE LANDMARKS OF YOUR LIFE

Correct Answers

1. We are to go into the world and preach the Gospel.
2. The Lord worked with them and confirmed the Word with signs following.
3. If we believe what we say shall come to pass, we can have whatever we say.
4. They gave a bad report saying that people were too strong.
5. They said that they should go up and possess the land for the Lord would give it into their hand.
6. They died by a plague.
7. Their corpses fell in the wilderness and they were not allowed to enter the land.
8. They would be brought into the land; however, they suffered for their father's unfaithfulness and wandered for 40 years in the wilderness.
9. He remained alive, took Moses' place as leader and led the children of Israel into the promised land and God granted him success.
10. He entered the land and possessed a mountain for his inheritance and was as strong at 80 as he was at 40.
11. Death and life are in the power of the tongue and man will be filled with the fruit of it.
12. We should fear lest we follow the same example and fail to enter.
13. Because it was not united by faith in those who heard.
14. She said, "If I may but touch His clothes, I shall be made whole."
15. She touched His clothes.
16. She felt in her body that she was healed.
17. She told what had happened.
18. He said, "This day the Lord will deliver you into my hand . . ."
19. He took a stone and slung it at the Philistine.
20. David received the victory over the Philistine.
21. He took the Philistine's head to Jerusalem.

"THE BOLD CONFESSORS OF THEIR FAITH"

Correct Answers

1. Our God whom we serve is able to deliver us from the fiery furnace but even if He does not, we will not serve or bow down before other gods.
2. They were thrown into the fiery furnace.
3. They were not burned, but were completely delivered.
4. a. They put their trust in God.
   b. They violated the King's command.
   c. They yielded up their bodies so as not to serve foreign gods.
5. When Daniel knew the document was signed he entered his house and continued to kneel, pray and give thanks to God three times a day.
6. He was thrown into the lion's den and the den was sealed shut.
7. The angel of the Lord shut the mouth of the lions and he was not harmed.
8. a. He is the living God, enduring forever.
   b. His kingdom is one which will not be destroyed.
   c. His dominion will be forever.
   d. He delivers, rescues and performs signs and wonders in heaven and on earth.
9. You stiffnecked and uncircumcised in heart and ears, you always are resisting the Holy Spirit.
   Which one of the prophets did your fathers not persecute? They killed those who announced the Messiah's coming and you have become His, the Messiah's, murderer. Behold, I see the heavens open and the Son of Man standing at the right hand of God.
10. They stoned him to death.
11. The Lord did not hold the sin against them and a young man named "Saul" was forgiven so that he could be saved. Saul later became Paul the great apostle.
12. Through Paul (or Saul) the gospel was taken to the Gentiles.
13. By faith great victories were won and by faith men gave their lives for what they believed.
14. a. By the blood of the Lamb.
    b. By the word of their testimony.
    c. Loving not our lives unto death.

GOD'S PREDETERMINED PURPOSE
VERSUS
MAN'S FREE WILL

Correct Answers

1. God's ultimate plan will be established.
2. They rejected it.
3. a. To appoint a wife for Isaac.
   b. She had a choice.
4. God's will.
5. a. He was called to ministry and apostleship.
   b. He turned aside.
6. From Rebekah came a nation, and from that nation came the Messiah.
7. Life and prosperity or death and adversity.
8. Life and blessing.
9. No.
10. Appoint a king.
11. They were rejecting the Lord from being their King.
12. No.
13. Bondage and oppression.
14. They would cry and He would not answer.
15. Refused to listen.
16. He gave them their way—a king.
17. God.
18. Serve the Lord or act wickedly and be swept away.
19. To disobey.
20. He would have established his kingdom forever.
21. The kingdom was given to another.
22. To destroy all; he disobeyed.
23. God rejected him from his office as King.
24. He regretted that He had made Saul King.
25. To see what is in his heart—whether you will obey or not.
26. He gave it to someone else to fulfill.
27. For them to repent so He could forgive them.
28. They were not afraid; nor did they repent.
29. Go out and I will spare you.
30. He would build them up in the Lord; not to go to Egypt.
31. They went to Egypt and disobeyed.
32. If a people repents, God will change His mind.
33. Yes.
34. That it should never be destroyed.
35. Be diligent to make your calling sure.
36. a. Diligence in faith.
    b. Moral excellence.
    c. Knowledge.
    d. Self-control.
    e. Perseverance.
    f. Godliness.
    g. Brotherly kindness.
    h. Christian love.